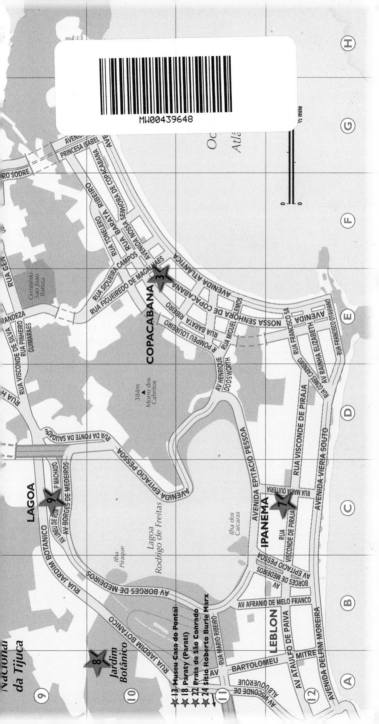

MW00439648

½ mile

Oc
Atlâ

**Nacional
da Tijuca**

9

LAGOA

P Machado

RUA JARDIM BOTÂNICO

AV BORGES DE MEDEIROS

AV MINEU DE ROM

Lagoa
Rodrigo de Freitas

Ilha
Piraque

Ilha dos
Caiçaras

Avenida Epitácio Pessoa

RUA DA FONTE DA SAÚDE

384m
Morro dos
Cabritos

AV HENRIQUE
DODSWORTH

RUA GEN

RUA VISCONDE DE SILVA

GRANDEZA

RUA PINHEIRO

GUIMARÃES

Cemitério
São João
Batista

RUA H

RUA SIQUEIRA CAMPOS

RUA FIGUEIREDO DE MAGALHÃES

RUA BARATA RIBEIRO

RUA TONELERO

AVENIDA NOSSA SENHORA DE COPACABANA

R POMPEU LOUREIRO

RUA BARATA RIBEIRO

NOSSA SENHORA DE COPACABANA

RUA MIGUEL LEMOS

AVENIDA ATLÂNTICA

AVENIDA
PRINCESA ISABEL

RO SODRE

COPACABANA 3

**JARDIM
BOTÂNICO** 8

IPANEMA 2

AV EPITÁCIO PESSOA

AV BORGES DE MEDEIROS

RUA MARIO RIBEIRO

AV

RUA JARDIM BOTÂNICO

AVENIDA EPITACIO PESSOA

RUA VISCONDE DE PIRAJA

RUA MARIA QUITÉRIA

RUA

RUA VISCONDE DE PIRAJA

AVENIDA VIEIRA SOUTO

RUA GOMES CARNEIRO

AV RAINHA ELIZABETH

RUA FRANCISCO SÁ

RUA FRANCISCO OTAVIANO

AVENIDA

LEBLON

AV AFRANIO DE MELO FRANCO

AVENIDA DELFIM MOREIRA

AV ATAULFO DE PAIVA

MITRE

AV VISCONDE DE
ALBUQUERQUE

BARTOLOMEU

AV

9

10

11

12

A

B

C

D

E

F

G

H

★ 13 Museu Casa do Pontal
★ 18 Paraty (Parati)
★ 22 Praia de São Conrado
★ 24 Sítio Roberto Burle Marx

Fodor's 25BEST
Rio de Janeiro

by Huw Hennessy

Fodor's Travel Publications
New York • Toronto • London • Sydney • Auckland
www.fodors.com

Contents

KEY TO SYMBOLS

- Map reference to the accompanying pull-out map
- Address
- Telephone number
- Opening/closing times
- Restaurant or café
- Nearest rail station
- Nearest Metrô (subway) station
- Nearest bus or tram route

- 🛥 Nearest boat or ferry stop
- ♿ Facilities for visitors with disabilities
- 🛈 Tourist information
- ❓ Other practical information

- 🏛 Admission charges: Expensive (over R$10), Moderate (R$6–R$10) and Inexpensive (under R$6)
- ▷ Further information

3

Introducing Rio de Janeiro

Rio de Janeiro is a city devoted to pleasure with exuberant high abandon. With its spectacular Carnaval, mania for sport, irrepressible love of music and dance, all played out against a gorgeous tropical backdrop, few would dispute Rio's credentials.

Rounded peaks clad in tropical forest overlook soft-sanded beaches on sweeping bays, which are lined with towering skyscrapers and colonial mansions. This magnificent natural setting forms one of the most stunning cityscapes on Earth. Add to this a year-round warm and balmy climate, and a history of cultural integration and tolerance, and it's easy to see why Rio is considered by its proud inhabitants and visitors to be one of the world's favourite cities.

Rio was the national capital and Imperial home for nearly two hundred years until, in 1960, it handed over to the purpose-built Brasília. (The old joke about the new capital city is that its most popular attraction is its weekend shuttle flight to Rio.) Some fine examples of Rio's architectural heritage have survived, but the modern city has stretched way beyond its original boundaries, blasting tunnels through the mountains to the beach neighbourhoods, followed by land reclamation projects pushing the shoreline back into Guanabara Bay.

For most *cariocas* (residents born in Rio), three elements are central to their lives: football, the beach and, perhaps most of all, music. From samba and bossa nova to the *baile funk* bass booming out from the *favelas* (shanty towns), music provides the pulse and passion in their hearts.

Although most visitors stay close to the Zona Sul beaches, Rio's attractions spread much further. Tropical islands, fringed with pristine beaches, dot the bay. Inland, forming a backdrop of jungle-clad mountains, is one of the largest urban national parks in the world, the Parque Nacional da Tijuca. This has the city's highest peak, Pico da Tijuca, which dwarfs the famous Sugarloaf and Corcovado mountains.

FACTS AND FIGURES

- Rio's highest mountain: Pico da Tijuca, 1,022m (3,353ft)
- Corcovado: 710m (2,329ft)
- Sugarloaf: 395m (1,296ft)
- Capacity of Estádio de Maracanã: 82,000 (but expansion planned for 2014)
- Height of Christ the Redeemer statue: 30m (98ft), excluding the pedestal
- Brazil's most popular national park: Tijuca, with 2 million visitors a year

LIPOTOURISM

Rio is widely considered the world capital of plastic surgery. The thriving so-called 'lipotourism' industry attracts US clients in particular, who combine a holiday in the sun with discreet nip-and-tuck operations, saving up to two-thirds on the typical medical costs back home. Brazil's eminence in plastic surgery is often attributed to pioneering surgeon Ivo Pitanguy, now in his eighties but still working.

OPEN ARMS

When locals first saw the Cristo Redentor statue looking over them from his high peak on Corcovado, some said that his outstretched arms meant that everyone is welcome in this warm-hearted city; others surmised he was shrugging in despair at their party lifestyle.

RIO'S MISNOMER

Sailing into the Baia de Guanabara on 1 January 1502, Portuguese explorer Gonçalo Coelho mistook the bay for a huge river mouth. He named the place River of January (Rio de Janeiro), a geographical error that has never been corrected.

Focus On Carnaval

Rio's Carnaval is a dazzling extravaganza that leaves rivals in the shade. The festivities surrounding the famous parades, leading up to Lent, are widely recognized as the world's greatest party. Life grinds to a halt for most of the week as *cariocas* and visitors from around the world sing, dance and make merry mayhem all night; then sleep it off on the beach until it's time to start again.

Origins

One of Carnaval's major influences is the samba—the blend of African drums, European dance and other elements that created the sensuous music so closely associated with Brazil. It wasn't until 1917, though, that samba was officially taken up by Rio's Carnaval, as the authorities at first shunned the lewd drum and dance rhythms pounding out from the poor dockside area. Its popularity spread rapidly across the city, with the formation of neighbourhood samba schools *(escolas de samba)*, each performing their own parade, the system still at the heart of today's contest.

Carnaval Today

More than all the countless other carnivals celebrated around Brazil, Rio's pageant is a huge commercial enterprise and the highlight of the city's calendar. It is still centred on the samba schools; the biggest and most famous are Mangueira and Portela, both of which have been crowned champions many times. Each school is composed of up to 3,000 costumed dancers, drummers and musicians, headed by the King and Queen. As well as performing its own song and dance, the school's floats represent a chosen theme—from outer-space travel to patriotic nostalgia. The victorious samba school wins a trophy, increased government funds for the whole neighbourhood, and the King—Rei Momo—gains the keys to the city.

Rio parties like no other city on Earth during Carnaval

In 1984 Carnaval's main event, the Samba Parade, moved to the Sambódromo, a purpose-built arena in the city centre, which is 1km (0.6 miles) long and allows some 70,000 people to watch the spectacle from its concrete terraces. For two consecutive nights, usually Sunday and Monday before Shrove Tuesday, the top 12 samba schools fill the Sambódromo with reverberating drums and a blaze of colour.

Planning Ahead

Tickets for the Samba Parade sell out months in advance and flights and hotels are at a premium. LIESA, the samba schools' league (http://liesa.globo.com; tel 3213 5151) is the cheapest place to buy tickets, but they usually sell out by December, after which try agencies such as Rio Carnaval Services (http://rio-carnival.net). Prices range from US$120 for the least expensive terrace seats to more than US$2,000 for VIP boxes.

In the weeks leading up to Carnaval, the city becomes increasingly festive, with top hotels hosting grand balls, and *blocos de rua* (samba groups) parading in massive street parties. One of the most popular parties is held in Ipanema, with members of the Banda de Ipanema (▷ 26) strutting their stuff. Samba schools hold rehearsals, which you can watch, though some of these take place in rough suburbs, so are best not visited alone. Many hotels arrange tours. You can see rehearsals of the main parades in the Sambódromo on most Saturdays from December; and the Cidade do Samba (▷ 67) has displays of Carnaval floats year-round.

Carnaval Dates and Websites

2012: 17–21 February
2013: 8–12 February
http://ipanema.com/carnival
http://rio-carnival.net

Whether it's in the Sambódromo or on the streets, the Carnaval spirit pervades the city during the celebrations

Top Tips For...

These great suggestions will help you tailor your ideal visit to Rio de Janeiro, no matter how you choose to spend your time.

...Offbeat Beaches

Escape the crowds at **Barra da Tijuca** (▷ 66), which stretches for 18km (11 miles) along the western outskirts.

Watch the hang-gliders land on the soft sands at **Praia Pepino** (▷ 57).

Be a castaway on jungle-clad **Ilha Grande**, off the Costa Verde (▷ 74).

...What's Free and Nearly Free

Hop on a *bonde* (tram; ▷ 58–59, 167) up to Santa Teresa.

Hike through lush forest trails in the **Parque Nacional da Tijuca** (▷ 50–51).

Hear northeastern Brazil's amazing range of musical styles at the **Feira de São Cristóvão** (▷ 67).

Ogle the artworks at the **Museu Nacional de Belas Artes** (▷ 42–43), Rio's top art gallery.

...Dancing 'til Dawn

Shimmy to some of Rio's best live samba bands at **Rio Scenarium** (▷ 136).

Mingle with Ipanema's beautiful people at **Baronneti** (▷ 132).

Hop from electronica to jazz in Barra's laidback **Nuth Lounge** (▷ 135).

...Full-on Action Sports

Hang-glide over the treetops of **São Conrado** (▷ 56–57), for the flight of your life.

Surf on the vast empty beaches of **Barra da Tijuca** (▷ 66).

Hike and climb in the **Parque Nacional Serra dos Orgãos** (▷ 74), home to some of Brazil's most challenging peaks.

Abseil down sparkling waterfalls in the **Tijuca National Park** (▷ 50–51).

Clockwise from top: Relaxing on the beach at Barra da Tijuca; a tasty Amazonian dish; descending from the summit of Pico da Tijuca; enjoying an evening drink in

...A Meal to Remember

Treat your tastebuds to Amazonian-French fusion cuisine at **Le Pré Catelan** (▷ 150).
Sample the city's best seafood in Ipanema's über-cool **Fasano al Mare** (▷ 147).
Feast on Brazil's national dish, *feijoada*, at the **Casa da Feijoada** (▷ 145).
Dine romantically under the stars in Santa Teresa's highly awarded **Aprazível** (▷ 142).

...Family Fun

Pose on top of a giant Carnaval float in the spectacular **Cidade do Samba** (▷ 67).
Whizz from tree to tree in the zip-wire jungle adventure in **Paraty** (▷ 75).
Play beach volleyball with the locals in **Ipanema** (▷ 26–27).

...Tropical Cruises

Paddle a kayak around tropical islets in **Paraty Bay** (▷ 75).
Sail around the idyllic **Ilha Grande** (▷ 74) on a traditional schooner.
Spy on sea turtles through a glass-bottomed catamaran in the sea at **Búzios** (▷ 14–15).

...Historic Architecture

Wander along the cobblestoned lanes of UNESCO-protected **Paraty** (▷ 48–49).
Visit **Petrópolis** (▷ 52–53), summer retreat of Emperor Dom Pedro II.
Be dazzled by the gold-leaf interior of **Mosteiro de São Bento** (▷ 34–35).
Climb to the much-loved **Igreja da Nossa Senhora da Glória do Outeiro** (▷ 24–25).

...Breathtaking Views

Watch the sun set over the city from **Pão de Açúcar** (▷ 46–47).
See Christ the Redeemer's lofty outlook from **Corcovado** (▷ 20–21).
Relax on the beaches at **Niterói** (▷ 44–45) and soak up the stunning views across the bay.

Paraty; the old tram climbs to Santa Teresa;
hang-gliders land on São Conrado's beach

Timeline

1500 Portuguese explorer Pedro Álvares de Cabral makes a chance landfall on the northeast coast of Brazil, and names his discovery the 'Island of the True Cross'.

1502 Gonçalo Coelho enters Guanabara Bay on 1 January and names the site Rio de Janeiro.

ORIGINS

Several indigenous tribes inhabited Guanabara Bay when the first European settlers arrived, including the Tamoio and the Tupinikin people. Many of the Portuguese married the local tribeswomen and formed families, creating a racial mix that is continued in present-day Rio de Janeiro.

MEET THE LOCALS

Rio's inhabitants are called *cariocas*, a name that is thought to have come from an indigenous term for the first settlers, *cari-oca*, which meant 'house of the whites'. Today a *carioca* defines someone who was born and raised in Rio de Janeiro, and with parents from the city.

1565 On 1 March, Portuguese commander Estácio de Sá founds the city of São Sebastião do Rio de Janeiro.

Late 1590s Boosted by settlers from Portugal, the city's population increases to nearly 4,000 inhabitants.

1690s The discovery of gold in Minas Gerais leads to a boom; the Novo Caminho is built, connecting Rio to Ouro Preto.

1763 Rio de Janeiro is made the new capital of Brazil. The estimated population is now 28,000 inhabitants.

1808 The Portuguese Royal Family arrives in Rio after being driven into exile by Napoleon. In 1815 they establish Rio as the Imperial capital.

1822 On 22 September, Dom Pedro declares the Independence of Brazil, with the rallying cry 'Independence or Death!'

A road linking Ouro Preto (above) with Rio was built in the late 17th century

A statue of Dom Pedro II on horseback

Rio was the capital of Brazil until 1960

1840s Mass development of coffee plantations in the hillsides around Rio and in the Paraíba do Sul Valley leads to the coffee boom era, which lasts until the 1870s.

1841 Dom Pedro II is crowned Emperor of Brazil.

1861–88 The reforestation of Tijuca Forest takes place (it had been cleared for farms and coffee plantations). More than 130,000 saplings are planted, establishing what becomes one of the largest urban national parks in the world.

1888 Slavery is abolished in Brazil.

Early 1900s Rio's population exceeds 500,000 inhabitants.

1907 An electric tramline is constructed around the city and up to Santa Teresa, over the iconic Arcos da Lapa viaduct.

1931 The Cristo Redentor statue is erected on Corcovado, in Tijuca National Park.

1950 The Maracanã Stadium is opened for the World Cup final, in which Uruguay defeats Brazil 2–1.

1960 Brasília replaces Rio de Janeiro as the new capital of Brazil.

1960s–70s Rio expands, with tunnels opening to the Zona Sul, land reclamation in Guanabara Bay and construction of the bridge to Niterói.

2012 Rio de Janeiro is due to host the UN Earth Summit on Sustainable Development.

2014 Brazil is due to stage the World Cup football tournament.

2016 Brazil has been chosen to host the Olympic Games.

SHANTY LIFE

An estimated fifth of Rio's population of five million inhabitants live in the city's notorious shanty towns, or *favelas*. Although many of these areas can be crime-ridden and dangerous, some offer tours and are considered hubs of musical and artistic creativity.

GOD'S OWN CITY?

The most acclaimed film to come out of Rio in recent years is *Cidade de Deus* (City of God). Fernando Meirelles' 2002 film portrays a violent gang living in the eponymous shanty town, and is based on an actual 1960s housing project that went wrong and became one of the city's most dangerous areas.

Top 25

This section contains the must-see Top 25 sights and experiences in Rio de Janeiro and the surrounding area. They are listed alphabetically, and numbered so you can locate them on the inside front cover map.

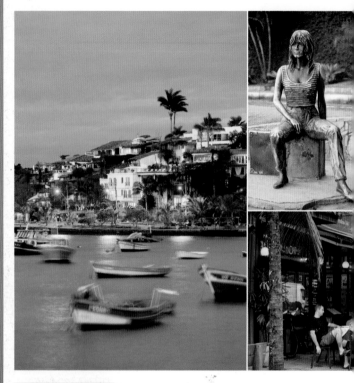

With its boutique hotels and cosmopolitan nightlife, Búzios is a magnet for trendy jet-setters. The sun-drenched peninsula also offers superb swimming in clean seas off more than 20 white-sand beaches.

Paradise discovered Officially called Armação dos Búzios, this upmarket beach resort lies some 180km (112 miles) east of Rio, on the Costa do Sol. Until the early 1960s, Búzios was a sleepy fishing village. Then, French actress Brigitte Bardot visited with her Brazilian boy-friend and the world rushed to join them in their tropical paradise. Today, a statue of Bardot sits on the promenade named after her. She looks wistfully over the beach, now dotted with parasols and pedaloes, to the schooners and the occasional cruise ship passing by.

Clockwise from far left: The harbour at dusk; a statue of Brigitte Bardot; pulling a boat to shore—Búzios was a quiet fishing village until tourism arrived; a scenic view of the harbour and town; a restaurant on Rua das Pedras

Laidback leisure... Tourism has now replaced fishing as the main occupation, but Búzios has largely retained its tranquillity, with small-scale developments only. The main centre, Rua das Pedras, is a rough-stoned street lined with small hotels, bars and boutiques, in whitewashed colonial buildings with tiled roofs. Most visitors are happy to spend the day on the beach, with Azeda, João Fernandinha and Ferradura among the best. Schooners take leisurely day trips around the coastline, with glass-bottomed boats revealing turtles and barracuda.

...or 24/7 action For more of an adrenalin rush, there's windsurfing, diving, surfing and kayaking, particularly on Ferradura and Brava beaches. By night, Rua das Pedras buzzes, with its cocktail bars and glitzy nightclubs.

THE BASICS

www.visitebuzios.com

🔲 Map, ▷ 111

🛈 Travessia dos Pescadores, corner of Praça Santos Dumont, tel (22) 2633 6200; daily 8am–10pm

🚌 3 hours from Rio, 10 departures daily, approx R$26 one-way (www.autoviacao1001.com.br)

HIGHLIGHTS

- Surfing
- Diving
- Snorkelling
- Rich marine life
- Forte São Mateus
- Sand dunes
- White-sand beaches

In contrast to its chic neighbour Búzios, Cabo Frio is a big and brash resort, its seafront packed with high-rise apartments and chain hotels. Its world-famous attraction, however, is Arraial do Cabo, whose clear waters are great for diving and snorkelling.

From pirates to surfers Cabo Frio endured a history of exploitation by the English, Dutch and French, with loggers and pirates competing for supremacy until the Portuguese took over in the 17th century. Today only ruins remain of the Forte São Mateus, but Cabo Frio has grown into a large modern resort, popular with weekenders from Rio, drawn to its miles of white-sand beaches and its water sports.

The town's main beach is Praia do Forte, named after the old Portuguese fort across the

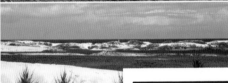

Clockwise from bottom left: A house in the resort's old town; colourful fishing boats wait for their owners to return; strolling on the sands; an old cannon stands guard on the Forte São Mateus; glistening-white sand dunes

bay. The flat expanse of soft sands and the calm, clean waters make the beach popular with families. Further east is Praia Brava, which has good waves for surfers, and beyond this is Praia Pero, backed by high sand dunes (beware of robberies—don't explore on your own).

Diving and snorkelling About 7km (5 miles) south down the coast is Arraial do Cabo, tucked inside a cove on the headland. With its sheltered waters, shipwrecks and cool currents attracting abundant marine life, it offers some of the best diving in Brazil. Favourite dive sites include Cordeiros, Porcos and Punta Leste, the last with particularly rich sea life, including barracuda, rays, turtles, moray eels, seahorses and coral. Snorkelling is also very good here, with the best beaches being Prainha and Forno.

THE BASICS

www.cabofrioturismo.rj.gov.br

🔳 Map, ▷ 111

🔒 Praça Cristóvão Colombo, Avenida Amérigo Vespúcio, tel (22) 2647 1689; Mon–Fri 9–5

🚌 1001 bus company, regular departures to Rio, 2 hours 40 min, approx R$25 one-way (www.autoviacao1001.com.br)

❓ Arraial do Cabo diving schools: PL Divers, tel (22) 2622 1033, www.pldivers.com.br; Sand'Mar Náutica, Rua Epitácio Pessoa 21, tel (22) 2622 5703, www.sandmar.com.br

DID YOU KNOW?

● The mosaic pavement on Copacabana's seafront was created in 1970 by Roberto Burle Marx (▷ 60). The pattern represents waves breaking on the shore.

TIPS

● Don't walk on the beach late at night; muggers and prostitutes are rife and it is dangerous.

● *Postos* (numbered one to five) are lifeguard stations, with cold showers and first-aid facilities. They fly red flags if the sea is too rough for bathing.

● Praia de Copacabana (3.5km/2 miles) becomes Praia do Leme at its eastern end, beyond the junction of Avenida Atlântica with Avenida Princesa Isabel.

Rio's best-known neighbourhood lives for and on its equally famous beach, a dazzling arc of soft sand, where joggers run in the early morning, tourists bake in the heat of the day, and kids play football after school.

Sleepy origins Before the first tunnel was blasted through the mountains in 1892, Copacabana was a quiet fishing village. Its popularity boomed in the 1920s with the opening of the Copacabana Palace Hotel, still Rio's most stately hotel. And when Fred Astaire and Ginger Rogers twinkle-toed through the 1933 musical *Flying Down to Rio*, the world followed in droves. With Carmen Miranda's tropical showgirl becoming Hollywood's symbol of a fun-loving *carioca*, Copacabana was established as everyone's favourite playground.

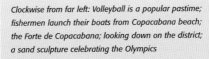

Clockwise from far left: Volleyball is a popular pastime; fishermen launch their boats from Copacabana beach; the Forte de Copacabana; looking down on the district; a sand sculpture celebrating the Olympics

Faded glory Today, the skyscrapers lining Avenida Atlântica confirm Copacabana's status as one of the most densely populated areas on the planet. Now, though, it is showing the strain of its enduring appeal, with formerly sparkling art deco facades looking a little careworn. Yet Copacabana still brims with top-class hotels and excellent restaurants, and its nightlife buzzes 24/7. New attractions are giving the area a facelift, including the Museu da Imagem e da Som (Museum of Image and Sound), on Avenida Atlântica.

Beach party On New Year's Eve, the beach fills with more than a million revellers for the Reveillon party. Live bands perform on giant stages and a firework display lights up the bay at the climax of exuberant festivities.

THE BASICS

⊞ E10

🛈 RioTur, Avenida Princesa Isabel 183, tel 2541 7522/2542 8004; Mon–Fri 9–6; with helpful, English-speaking staff

🚇 Cardeal Arcoverde, Siqueira Campos, Praça General Osório

🚌 123, 125, 132, 570, 572

The statue of Christ the Redeemer on Corcovado is Rio's most stunning image. The ride up the mountain and the breathtaking views over the city are an unmissable experience on anyone's agenda.

First visitors Dom Pedro II ordered the construction of the railway to Corcovado and in 1885 a steam train carried the first visitors up the steep mountainside. With the addition of Cristo Redentor nearly 50 years later, Rio found its most iconic symbol. The elegant art deco statue was assembled on site and inaugurated on 12 October 1931.

Lofty outlook From its pedestal atop the hunchbacked peak, Cristo Redentor commands an unmatched view over Zona Sul's landmarks:

Clockwise from far left: Looking down from Corcovado over central Rio, towards the Rio-Niterói bridge; Sugarloaf mountain, as seen from the statue; Christ's outstretched arms; a view of Corcovado and its iconic statue, with Sugarloaf in the distance

Copacabana, Ipanema, Lagoa Rodrigo de Freitas and Jardim Botânico; and inland to the Maracanã and beyond. Corcovado receives more than one million visitors a year, so you're unlikely to find solitude. Check the weather before setting off, as cloud sometimes shrouds the peak all day. If you wait until late afternoon (with fewer crowds), you'll be rewarded with the spectacle of floodlights (switched on at dusk), bathing the statue in a golden hue.

Ride or walk The funicular railway, which climbs slowly up through lush vegetation, is the best way to get to the top. But if you fancy a walk, the train stops at the Paineiras station, from where there is a scenic trail (about 3km/2 miles) past waterfalls, and with a detour to the Dona Marta lookout point.

THE BASICS

www.corcovado.com.br

✚ C8 (Cristo Redentor statue); D7 (Cosme Velho station)

🍴 Two cafés at Cosme Velho station and Corcovado ($)

🚌 180, 584

🚈 Corcovado Train (Trem do Corcovado) starts at Cosme Velho station (Rua Cosme Velho 513) and takes you up to Corcovado station, for the statue. Tel 2558 1329; trains daily 8.30–6.30, every 30 min

♿ Few (escalators and lift to foot of statue)

💲 Expensive

HIGHLIGHTS

● Local matches between Botafogo, Flamengo, Vasco da Gama and Fluminense
● Stadium visit, including football stars' footprints and the throne used by Pope John Paul II and Queen Elizabeth II

TIP

● The stadium will be closed in 2012 as renovations take place in preparation for the 2014 World Cup Finals. It is due to reopen some time in 2013. Matches will be held at alternative venues.

This is the undisputed home of Brazilian football and was once the world's biggest soccer stadium. As well as hosting the 2014 World Cup Finals, the Maracanã also stages concerts and events, with past names including Frank Sinatra and Pope John Paul II.

World Cup debut Officially called the Estádio Jornalista Mario Filho, but best known as the Maracanã, the stadium was built in 1950 when Brazil first hosted the World Cup Finals. A world-record 200,000 spectators saw Uruguay beat Brazil 2–1 in the final, plunging the city into a state of shock. When full seating was installed, capacity reduced to 82,000, but an expansion to 90,000 is planned for 2014, when the World Cup will again be held here.

Clockwise from far left: The Maracanã is already a vast stadium, but expansion is planned for the World Cup in 2014; Botafogo fans pack the stands; Flamengo supporters cheer on their team

Lasting impressions The Maracanã has witnessed many football milestones, including Pele's 1,000th goal, which he scored for Santos against Vasco in 1969. More than 90 of the stadium's most famous players have been immortalized in the Calçada da Fama (Stars' Pavement), seen during tours, with footprints including those of Pele, Jairzinho and Zico.

In the crowd Watching a match here is one of Rio's highlights—football fan or not. State and national league seasons run throughout most of the year, with particular excitement focused on the finals held at the Maracanã in early May. Expect carnivalesque goal celebrations, especially during local derbies between Rio's top teams—Botafogo, Flamengo, Fluminense and Vasco da Gama—all of whom play here.

THE BASICS

www.suderj.rj.gov.br/maracana.asp

🟦 A3

✉ Rua Professor Eurico Rabelo, Maracanã

☎ 2334 1705 (Visitor Centre)

🕐 Daily 9–5 (but closed in 2012 for renovations; ▷ Tip)

🍴 Snack bars ($)

🚇 Maracanã

♿ Few

💰 Moderate

❓ Museum (Gate 18) daily 9.30–5, match days 8am–11am; moderate entry fee

6 Igreja da Nossa Senhora da Glória do Outeiro

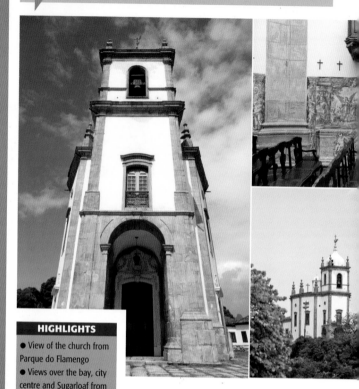

- View of the church from Parque do Flamengo
- Views over the bay, city centre and Sugarloaf from the courtyard
- 17th-century *azulejo* tiles
- 19th-century carved woodwork

TIPS

- It's a steep walk up to the church; alternatively, take the free 'Plano Inclinado' elevator from Rua do Russell 312.
- 15 August is the Day of Our Lady of Glória, with a special Mass and a parade of the Virgin, plus street stalls and music.

Perched on the edge of a hill overlooking Guanabara Bay, Nossa Senhora da Glória do Outeiro is one of the most picturesque colonial churches in Rio, its dainty white outline rising above the treetops. There are wonderful views from its courtyard.

Small but well loved *Cariocas* have always had a special fondness for this beautiful little 17th-century church, whose site is historically important to the city. Captain Estácio de Sá, who in 1565 established the first Portuguese settlement in Rio, claimed this hilltop *(outeiro)* as his first victory over the French colonists. Dom Pedro I and Dona Leopoldina chose the church to baptize their children, beginning with their eldest daughter, Maria da Glória, in 1819.

Clockwise from far left: The church dates from the 17th century; inside, blue-and-white azulejos (tiles) show scenes from the Bible; the carved woodwork is another highlight; the church, surrounded by greenery and with Corcovado as a backdrop

Inside and out Completed in 1739, the simple design of Nossa Senhora da Glória is attributed to Portuguese military architect José Cardoso Ramalho. Based around two inter-connected octagonal shapes, the church is topped by an onion-shaped cupola over the single bell tower, with an arched portico in front of the main entrance. Inside, the church is richly decorated in a style spanning the rococo and neoclassical periods. Blue-and-white faience-style *azulejos* (tiles) cover most of the lower walls, painted with Bible scenes. The paintings are attributed to prominent 17th-century Brazilian painter Mestre Valentim Almeida. Ornately carved woodwork in the choir, chancel and altar was largely added in the 19th century. Behind the church is the Museu Mauro Ribeiro Viegas, with paintings and religious artefacts.

THE BASICS

www.outeirodagloria.org.br

☩ G4

✉ Praça Nossa Senhora da Glória, Glória

☎ 2225 2869

🕐 Church: Mon–Fri 9–5, Sat–Sun 9–12. Museum: Tue–Fri 9–5, Sat 9–12, Sun 9–1

🚇 Glória

🚌 172

♿ None

🎫 Free

❓ Guided tours first Sun of the month, by prior arrangement only

HIGHLIGHTS

- Beach volleyball
- Hippy Market
- Sunset over Dois Irmãos and Pedra da Gávea peaks
- Rua Vinicius de Moraes
- Rua Visconde de Pirajá

TIP

- Banda de Ipanema is the best-known gay-friendly Carnaval band and it famously attracts some outrageously dressed drag queens. It meets on Praça General de Osório on the Saturday two weeks before Carnaval and on Carnaval Saturday and Tuesday, with hundreds of visitors joining in the fun street parade.

This has been Rio's trendiest beach district ever since 1964, when Vinicius de Moraes penned 'The Girl from Ipanema' about one particular beauty who frequented the sands. With their chic bars and clubs, Ipanema's beautiful people are still turning heads.

Beach chic While Copacabana has slumped recently, Ipanema has retained its superior tag, with its chic boutique hotels, gourmet restaurants and oh-so cool cocktail bars. The streets are narrower, with fewer cars, there are more outdoor cafés on tree-lined pavements, and the area has a more refined feel.

Pick your *posto* Ipanema's beach is still the main attraction, with distinct sections claimed by different groups: Surfers catch the big

Clockwise from far left: Ipanema's famous beach stretches into the distance; looking inland towards the mountains; cycling along the seafront; locals and visitors alike enjoy the beach; fruit and vegetables on sale in the local market

waves at *posto* 7 (Arpoador); the stretch between *posto* 8 and *posto* 9 is favoured by gays; *posto* 9 is the most fashionable hot spot; beach volleyball is concentrated around *posto* 10; and the gentler waves at *posto* 11 in adjacent Leblon draw young families.

From malls to markets Rua Visconde de Pirajá is the busiest commercial strip, with speciality stores, boutiques and late-night book-shops; Rua Vinicius de Moraes is full of lively bars, shops and restaurants. Don't miss the Sunday Hippy Market on Praça General Osório.

Sun worshippers Sunset-watching is a social event. Locals gather on the beach to witness the golden light sinking and may even applaud a particularly impressive spectacle.

THE BASICS

➕ C12

📍 Praça General Osório

🚌 123, 125, 132, 569, 571, 573, 570, 572

⭐ **8** Jardim Botânico

The magnificently lush, green Botanical Gardens offer a peaceful retreat from the sun-baked beaches, with shady avenues, fountains, statues and ornamental ponds.

By royal invitation Emperor Dom João VI founded the Jardim Botânico in 1808, as a nursery for cultivating herbs, tea and spices imported from Asia, exclusively for the Royal Family. It wasn't until 1822 that the gardens opened to the public, with the addition of ponds and scenic walkways, and the introduction of a huge range of plants.

Birds and monkeys Today, it is one of the world's most important botanical gardens, with 8,000 species of plants, growing in natural habitat areas and glasshouses. Look for

Clockwise from bottom left: Giant water lilies in the Lago Frei Leandro; the Fountain of the Muses; beautiful orchids are among the many flowers you'll find here; the Museu Casa dos Pilões displays items relating to when the site hosted a gunpowder factory

orchids, bromeliads and giant ferns and cacti; plus colourful parrots, hummingbirds, butterflies and monkeys feeding in the vegetation.

Giant water lilies and towering palms The site covers an area equivalent to about 137 football pitches, so it's worth spending several hours enjoying it properly. A good place to start is the Gruta Karl Glasl, from where you can see the giant water lilies in the adjacent pond and look across the gardens to the statue of Cristo Redentor. The most famous area is the Avenida das Palmas Imperiais—a long avenue shaded by 200 Imperial Palms, towering trees grown from one single specimen planted in the early 19th century. Some of the original buildings have been preserved; the Visitor Centre is in a former sugar mill.

THE BASICS

www.jbrj.gov.br

➕ A10

✉ Rua Jardim Botânico 1008, Jardim Botânico

☎ 3874 1808

🕐 Daily 8–5

🍴 Café ($$)

🚌 170, 571, 572

♿ Few wheelchair facilities; sensory garden

💷 Inexpensive

❓ Guided tours in English from the Visitor Centre. Also tours for visitors with special needs and the over-60s; booking is essential, call in advance

9 Lagoa

HIGHLIGHTS

- Swan pedaloes on the lagoon
- Cycling around the lake
- Lakeside cafés
- Fundação Eva Klabin
- Parque da Catacumba
- Jockey Club
- Instituto Moreira Salles

DID YOU KNOW?

- The world's tallest floating Christmas tree, 85m (279ft) high, is built on a raft on Lagoa Rodrigo de Freitas every Christmas.

This smart residential neighbourhood is tucked inland behind Ipanema, around the shores of Lagoa Rodrigo de Freitas. Although not on the main tourist trail, it has fine restaurants, museums and parks, as well as leisure activities on the lagoon.

Pleasure lagoon The heart of Lagoa is its broad expanse of water, the Lagoa Rodrigo de Freitas, connected to the sea via the canal dividing Ipanema and Leblon beaches. The lagoon is well used by locals and visitors alike, with several sailing clubs, as well as the swan-shaped pedaloes available for hire from its southeastern corner (opposite the junction of *avenidas* Epitácio Pessoa and Henrique Dodsworth). One of the most popular Sunday afternoon family activities is to paddle around

Clockwise from far left: The path around the lagoon is popular with joggers; admiring the view across the water; you can take to the water on a swan-shaped pedalo; looking down on Lagoa Rodrigo de Freitas

in a pedalo, followed by a coconut milk or smoothie at a lakeshore kiosk. About 25 snack bars and restaurants ring the lagoon, offering everything from a hot dog to Amazonian fish soup at the award-winning thatch-roofed Palaphita Kitch (Quiosco 20, Avenida Epitácio Pessoa, daily 6pm–3am). Joggers and cyclists use the track around the lagoon's perimeter.

From art to horse racing Lagoa is also a cultural hub, with several art galleries, most notably the Instituto Moreira Salles (▷ 68) and the superb Fundação Eva Klabin (▷ 68). On the western shore is the Jockey Club, Rio's main horse-racing track. One of Rio's best antiques markets, the Feira de Antigüedades (▷ 121) takes place on Sundays in the nearby Praça Santos Dumont.

THE BASICS

➕ C9

🍴 A good choice of snack bars and restaurants ($–$$$)

🚇 Cantagalo

🚌 571, 573, 583

❓ If you tire of the beach there are several excellent parks nearby: Parque da Catacumba (➕ D11), Jardim Botânico (▷ 28–29) and Parque da Cidade (▷ 72). There are bike-hire companies at several points around the lagoon

With its landmark two-tiered Arcos da Lapa, this is Rio's most vibrant bohemian neighbourhood. Lapa's nightclubs offer the best live-music scene, with everything from bossa-nova and jazz to funk.

Humble origins A network of narrow streets between the city centre and the bay, in its early years Lapa was a squalid, disease-ridden place, overrun with brigands and brothels. It also attracted artists and writers, however, and since the 1950s its bohemian character has taken hold. Today, Lapa has smartened up its colonial facades and converted former factories into clubs and bars, transforming the neighbourhood into Rio's most dynamic music scene. If you've got the energy, you can spend the whole night hopping from place to place.

Clockwise from top left: Browsing the stalls in the Feira do Rio Antigo antiques market; a bonde tram travels up to Santa Teresa; enjoying an evening drink in an outdoor café on Rua do Lavradio; the Igreja da Nossa Senhora da Lapa; a tram crosses the Arcos da Lapa

Arcos da Lapa The delicate white arches of the Arcos da Lapa stand out beside the modern cathedral (▷ 66) and the monolithic Petrobras building. Built as an aqueduct to bring water to the city, it now carries the open-sided *bonde* trams (▷ 58). Under the arches are the entertainment venues Circo Voador (▷ 133) and Fundição Progresso (▷ 134).

From antiques to mosaics On the first Saturday of the month, the Rua do Lavradio hosts a lively antiques market, the Feira do Rio Antigo (▷ 123), with samba bands playing late into the evening. Nearby streets have antiques shops and *boteco* bars. On the other side of the Arcos is the Escadaria Selarón pavement mosaic (▷ 67). Nearby, the Sala Cecília Meireles (▷ 136) hosts chamber music.

THE BASICS

www.lanalapa.com.br
🔢 G3
🍴 Restaurants, bars and cafés ($–$$$)
🚇 Cinelândia
🚃 Tram to Carioca

HIGHLIGHTS

● Gold-leaf interior
● 17th-century icons of Nossa Senhora Monserrate, São Bento and Santa Escolastica
● Gregorian chants at Sunday Mass

TIPS

● No photography is allowed inside the church.
● Appropriate clothing should be worn—no shorts or bare shoulders.

This precious 17th-century church and Benedictine monastery stand on a hilltop overlooking the city centre. Though the church's facade is plain, its extravagantly decorated interior is ablaze with gold leaf.

Benedictine founders One of the most important examples of religious architecture of its kind in Brazil, the Mosteiro de São Bento was founded in 1590 by Benedictine monks from Bahia, northeastern Brazil. From its vantage point just off the northern end of Avenida Rio Branco, São Bento offers a peaceful retreat from the commercial bustle below, with glimpses of the bay and docks from its tree-lined courtyard. Access is from Rua Dom Gerardo either via a lift (free) or at the end of the winding road.

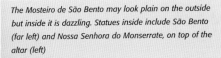

The Mosteiro de São Bento may look plain on the outside but inside it is dazzling. Statues inside include São Bento (far left) and Nossa Senhora do Monserrate, on top of the altar (left)

Dazzling interior The twin-towered church itself is thought to date from 1719, the design attributed to Portuguese architect Francisco de Frias Mesquita. Its exterior is plain and simple, but the magnificence of the building is focused on the dazzling gold leaf, which coats all the interior walls, carved wooden chapels and the barrel-vaulted ceiling. The eight chapels flanking the central nave are dedicated to different saints. One of Rio's most acclaimed rococo sculptors, Inácio Ferreira Pinto, created much of the church's finest work, at the end of the 18th century. The altar is headed by a carving of Nossa Senhora do Monserrate, after whom the church was originally named. The adjoining monastery is not generally open to visitors, as it still houses Benedictine monks, who follow an order of silence.

THE BASICS

www.osb.org.br

➕ G1

✉ Rua Dom Gerardo 68, Centro

☎ 2206 8100

🕐 Daily 7–6

Ⓜ Uruguaiana

🚌 123, 125, 132 to Avenida Rio Branco

♿ Few (lift from street)

💲 Free

❓ Tours (English/Spanish/Portuguese) Mon–Sat 9–4 (30 min). Monks sing Gregorian chants on Sun during Mass (10am)

12 Museu de Arte Moderna

HIGHLIGHTS

- *Urutu* by Tarsila do Amaral
- *O Farol* by Anita Malfatti
- *Mademoiselle Pogany II* by Constantin Brancusi

TIPS

- Take care crossing the busy Avenida Presidente Wilson and use the footbridge over Avenida Infante Dom Henrique from Rua João Neves da Fontoura.
- Take advantage of the discounted family ticket on Sundays: up to five people for the price of one adult.
- Free live music events take place on Sundays, 11.30am in the cinema.

Rio's leading modern art museum stands out on the green space of Burle Marx's Parque do Flamengo, the reclaimed strip of land running alongside Praia do Flamengo. The outstanding art collection is complemented by temporary exhibitions, film screenings and workshops.

Striking building The museum, known as MAM, is in a light, airy building designed by Brazilian architect Affonso Eduardo Reidy. It comprises a rectangular shell suspended above ground by v-shaped concrete supports. Smoked-glass windows offer views of Glória Marina and draw diffused light into the galleries.

Reborn from the fire Inaugurated in 1958, MAM was devastated by a fire in 1978 that

Far left: The striking building was designed by Brazilian architect Affonso Eduardo Reidy; Left: Apocalipse by Gustavo Speridião; Below: Artworks on display, left to right: Sem título by Otavio Schipper, Sem título by Presto, Auto-retrato (Self-portrait) by Alex Cabral, Sem título by Paulo Campinho

destroyed nearly all of its exhibits, including priceless works by Picasso and Dali. Art collector Gilberto Chateaubriand came to the rescue in 1993, donating his entire collection of some 4,000 pieces. It is considered the most valuable treasury of modern Brazilian art in existence.

An impressive roll-call Today, MAM has re-established its status as one of Brazil's leading museums, with some 11,000 permanent exhibits by Brazilian artists including Anita Malfatti, Tarsila do Amaral, Lasar Segall, Di Cavalcanti, Ismael Nery and Cândido Portinari. International artists represented include Jean Arp, Constantin Brancusi, Alberto Giacometti, Fernand Léger and Henry Moore. The film collection is one of the largest in Latin America.

THE BASICS

www.mamrio.org.br

✚ G3

✉ Avenida Infante Dom Henrique 85, Parque do Flamengo

☎ 2240 4944. Cinema: 2240 4913

🕐 Tue–Fri 12–6, Sat–Sun 1–7

🍴 Restaurant/bar ($$)

Ⓜ Cinelândia

🚌 154, 438, 472

♿ Good

💵 Inexpensive

❓ Small bookshop in the entrance hall; Novo Disenho design shop next to the museum

13 Museu Casa do Pontal

HIGHLIGHTS

● Musical trio
● Carnaval parade
● Circus scene
● Festival costumes
● Puppets

DID YOU KNOW?

● The Casa do Pontal has been recognized by UNESCO's International Council of Museums as 'not just a complete museum of Brazilian Popular Art but a true anthropological museum'.

This folk-art museum houses an enchanting collection of craft figures made by more than 200 artists from across Brazil. The 5,000 wooden and ceramic pieces are arranged by theme, illustrating everyday life: work, play, festivals, sport and religion.

A disappearing world French designer and collector Jacques van de Beuque (1922–2000) emigrated to Brazil after World War II and travelled around the country for 40 years, collecting hundreds of figurines, some tiny and others life-sized. His collection has been arranged here in enchanting tableaux: a convoy of mule carts, a barber shaving a customer, a woman pounding cassava in a pestle and mortar, children playing games, cowboys on horseback, football spectators in a stadium.

The museum, surrounded by greenery

Some of the fascinating exhibits inside

Fantastical scenes include rows of little houses elaborately carved into the roots of a tree. The museum is one of Rio's unmissable cultural gems, offering an insight into a traditional way of life that is fast disappearing.

In motion The displays will delight children as much as adults, with several scenes animated at the push of a button: a trio of musicians, a mechanic's workshop, a Carnaval parade and a circus, complete with tightrope walkers and dancing animals. For adults only, there's even a small collection of erotic figures, discreetly tucked away in a separate room.

Other activities The museum also stages temporary exhibitions and hosts seminars on a range of topics.

THE BASICS

www.museucasadopontal.
com.br

🔳 Map, ▷ 104 a4

✉ Estrada do Pontal
3295, Recreio dos
Bandeirantes

☎ 2490 3278

🕐 Tue–Sun 9.30–5

🍴 Café ($)

🚌 175, 179 from Zona
Sul to Barra Shopping;
703 to Estrada do Pontal

♿ Few

💲 Moderate

❓ Tours by appointment
(Tue–Fri); gift shop

HIGHLIGHTS

● Feathered headdresses
● Carved wooden animals
● Artindia handicrafts shop
● Photographic displays in the garden
● Indian rituals on video and sound recordings

TIPS

● Children should love the hands-on activities, such as face-painting, as well as the multimedia special effects.
● Special events take place at the museum on 19 April, the Day of the Indian in Brazil.

This superb museum, managed by FUNAI, the National Indian Foundation, focuses on Brazil's rich indigenous cultural heritage. From the Amazon Basin to the border of Paraguay, an estimated 650,000 indigenous people belong to some 220 ethnic tribes.

The collections In addition to maintaining its archive collection, the Museu do Índio holds long- and short-term exhibitions, focusing on groups such as the Guaraní in the south-east and the Oiapoque in northern Brazil. Long-term exhibitions are shown in the main building—the Casarão. The courtyard garden is used for live events, including music and dance festivals. There are temporary exhibitions in the art gallery, and photographic displays are mounted on outside walls.

Clockwise from far left: A Guaraní Indian; traditional crafts are displayed at the museum; feathered headdresses are among the highlights of the collection; colourful baskets

Astral ritual One exhibition, 'Presence of the Invisible', is devoted to the Oiapoque, who inhabit the far northern state of Amapá. Inside the Casarão, a glowing blue light in the star-studded ceiling illuminates feathered upright poles forming the perimeter of a traditional *Turé* cosmological ritual.

Sounds of the rainforest Galleries display wooden carvings, costumes, ceramics, weapons and woven baskets. Ambient sound recordings and film clips vividly recreate daily life in the rainforest, from dance and prayers to fishing and hunting. A thatched wooden building contains the Artindia shop, selling items bought direct from Indian communities. These include woven baskets, jewellery, musical instruments, books and CDs.

THE BASICS

www.museudoindio.gov.br
➕ E8
✉ Rua das Palmeiras 55, Botafogo
☎ 3214 8700
🕐 Tue–Fri 9–5.30, Sat–Sun 1–5
🍴 Café ($)
🚇 Botafogo
🚌 172, 511, 512
♿ Good
🎟 Inexpensive (free Sun)

HIGHLIGHTS

● Brazilian sculptures on the second floor
● *Primera Missa no Brasil (The First Mass in Brazil,* 1860), by Victor Meirelles
● *Auto-Retrato (Self-Portrait,* 1923) by Tarsila do Amaral
● *Café (Coffee,* 1935) by Cândido Portinari

TIP

● Visit the museum on Sunday, when entry is free and the Metrô less busy.

This is the most important art museum in Rio, based on a collection brought to Brazil by Emperor Dom Joao VI. The superb display of European art has been supplemented with fine 19th- and 20th-century Brazilian paintings and sculptures.

European inspiration Housed in a classical building close to the entertainment district Cinelândia, the original art collection of some 800 pieces was brought from Europe in 1808 by the fleeing Portuguese Royal Family, with the aim of stimulating a new artistic culture within Brazil. It was added to in 1816, with French artist Joachim Lebreton acquiring 50 pieces from Italy, Holland and France, covering the 16th to 18th centuries; and subsequently built up to form part of the newly created

Clockwise from bottom left: Café, by Cândido Portinari (1935); looking down the elegant sculpture gallery; the building housing the museum dates from the early 20th century; sculptures on display

Royal School of Art. The building was designed (1906–08) by Spanish architect Adolfo Morales de los Ríos. It now contains more than 16,000 works spread over three floors, including paintings, sculpture, engravings, furniture, African art and folk art.

Artistic masterpieces The highlights are considered to be the artworks from the late 19th and early 20th centuries, with paintings by international artists, including impressionists Alfred Sisley and Louis Eugène Boudin, and modernists Chagall and Picasso; as well as some of the finest masterpieces by leading Brazilian artists, including Victor Meirelles, Agostinho da Mota, Belmiro de Almeida, Rodolfo Amoedo, Eliseu Visconti, Tarsila do Amaral, Di Cavalcanti and Cândido Portinari.

THE BASICS

www.mnba.gov.br

⊞ G3

✉ Avenida Rio Branco 199, Centro

☎ 2219 8474

🕐 Tue–Fri 10–6, Sat–Sun 12–5

🚇 Cinelândia

🚌 123, 125, 132

♿ Few

💰 Inexpensive

HIGHLIGHTS

● Museu de Arte
Contemporânea
● Parque da Cidade
● Fortaleza de Santa Cruz
da Barra
● Caminho Niemeyer
● Icaraí restaurants

TIPS

● Linha de Turismo buses
link Niterói's highlights.
The buses, with English-
speaking guides, depart
from Praça Araribóia on
Saturdays, Sundays and
holidays at 10, 12.30 and
2.30; R$10 one-way.
● A bridge 13km (8 miles)
long links Niterói to Rio
across the bay.

The old joke about Niterói is that the best
thing about it is its view of Rio across the
bay. While the views are magnificent, this
city of nearly 500,000 people does have a
few other things to shout about, including
a futuristic art museum, a colonial fortress
and a jungle-clad, mountain-top park.

Architectural wonders After Brasília, Niterói
has the country's greatest concentration
of buildings designed by Oscar Niemeyer,
Brazil's foremost modern architect. These
buildings together make up the Caminho
Niemeyer, or Niemeyer Way. The Museu de
Arte Contemporânea, founded in 1996, is
one of Niemeyer's most stunning buildings, its
curvaceous outlines emulating Rio's rounded
peaks. The museum has some 1,200 works

Clockwise from top left: The eye-catching Museu de Arte Contemporânea (MAC); strolling along Charitas beach; looking out over Niterói from Sugarloaf mountain; relaxing on Itacoatiara beach

of 20th-century Brazilian art. The oval building is perched on a slim support over a pond. The courtyard beneath looks across the bay to Rio and along Niterói's coastline to the Fortaleza de Santa Cruz da Barra, a historic colonial fort.

Beaches and restaurants Just beyond the Art Museum is Icaraí, Niterói's main shopping district. A string of restaurants faces the beach, but the polluted water is not recommended for swimming. Farther around the coast, however, are several beaches facing the open sea, which are clean and good for surfing, particularly Praia Itacoatiara.

Hang-gliders' perch Overlooking Icaraí is the Parque da Cidade, with miles of forest trails. At the park's summit are two hang-glider ramps.

THE BASICS

www.neltur.com.br

🔢 Map, ▷ 111; also B1 inset on pull-out map

🛈 Neltur, Estrada Leopoldo Fróes 773, Niterói, tel (21) 2710 2727; daily 9–5

🚌 741 from Copacabana to Charitas ferry terminal

⛴ From Praça XV to Charitas ferry terminal

Museu de Arte Contemporânea

www.macniteroi.com.br

✉ Mirante de Boa Viagem, Boa Viagem, Niterói

☎ (21) 2620 2400

🕐 Tue–Sun 10–6; courtyard daily 9–6

🍴 Restaurant ($$), café ($)

🚌 Rodoviário Niterói (the bus station) is a 15-min walk from the museum

♿ Few

💲 Inexpensive

HIGHLIGHTS

● Sunset over Rio from the summit of Pão de Açúcar
● Tropical wildlife
● Film show
● Scenic picnic sites
● Antique cable car
● Views from the glass-walled cable cars

DID YOU KNOW?

● The first recorded climber to conquer Pão de Açúcar was Englishwoman Henrietta Carstairs, in 1817.
● The peak's first cable car was launched in 1912. A replica of the original car stands on Morro da Urca.
● Former passengers have included Albert Einstein, John F. Kennedy, Sophia Lauren and Brooke Shields.

Up to 2,000 people a day take the cable car up Pão de Açúcar (Sugarloaf), making it one of Rio's most popular attractions. Riding the glass-walled capsules is an aerial adventure, with stunning views.

Take-off From the main station, by Praia Vermelha in Urca, you soar up Morro da Urca, the smaller peak adjacent to Pão de Açúcar, rising to 220m (727ft) above sea level. Vantage points offer views across the bay to the city centre, and west to Copacabana and the beaches beyond. There are cafés, restaurants, shops, a film theatre and even a heliport.

Ancient rocks Enormous, bare-domed Morro da Urca and Pão de Açúcar are composed of granite-based rock, dating back some 600

Clockwise from far left: Sugarloaf looms over the marina; the views at sunset are stunning; the cable-car ride to the top of the mountain is a memorable experience; tourists take in the views

million years. The massif is fringed with lush vegetation, remnants of the rainforest that once covered the coastline. If you're lucky, you might spot toucans, parrots, monkeys and butterflies flitting through the trees.

Reaching the summit From Morro da Urca you hop on another cable car for the second leg of the journey, a span of some 750m (2,460ft) up to the summit of Pão de Açúcar, 395m (1,296ft) above the ocean. A 360-degree panorama takes in the whole city—Corcovado rising above Tijuca National Park, across the bay to Niterói and, on a clear day, as far as the fingerlike peaks of Dedo do Deus on the horizon to the north. Paths and picnic sites offer more opportunities to soak up the breathtaking setting.

THE BASICS

www.bondinho.com.br

🔶 J8

✉ Avenida Pasteur 520, Urca

☎ 2461 2700

🕐 Daily 8–7.50

🍴 Restaurants and snack bars ($–$$)

🚇 Botafogo

🚌 107, 511, 512

♿ Few

💲 Expensive

❓ Check out the new cable-car museum on Morro da Urca

HIGHLIGHTS

- Boat cruises
- View from Forte Defensor Perpétuo
- Jungle nature hikes
- Gold Trail
- Colonial architecture
- Arts and handicrafts

TIP

- Paraty comes over all bookish every July for FLIP—*Festival Literária Internacional de Paraty*. The literary festival attracts top writers, with debates, readings and launches of new titles. Visit www.flip.org.br for details.

This little port squeezed up against the Mata Atlântica—Coastal Atlantic Forest—is one of the most picturesque places in Brazil. Its old quarter is a timeless grid of whitewashed colonial houses lining narrow cobbled streets.

Founded in gold Paraty developed at the turn of the 17th century as the port for gold, diamonds and emeralds brought down from Minas Gerais. Churches were founded, fortresses built to fend off pirates, and the town prospered until the 19th century, when a new railway opened, linking São Paulo to Rio, leaving Paraty isolated. Paraty's colonial heritage has been preserved, however, supported by a flow of visitors along the breathtaking Costa Verde highway.

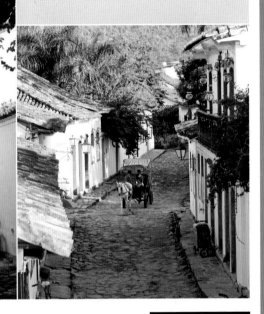

Paraty's old town is a charming blend of cobbled streets and whitewashed houses, with the forest-clad slopes of the Mata Atlântica rising steeply in the background

Traffic-free old quarter Paraty's old town has cobblestone streets lined with handicraft shops, art galleries, cafés and *pousadas*. Its oldest churches, with their beautiful bell towers, are on the main squares and seafront.

Views and activities On the edge of Paraty, crossing the Rio Perequê-Açu, remains of the old colonial Forte Defensor Perpétuo provide great views over the bay. But Paraty is best seen from the sea, with the sheer forest wall rising up behind. You can take a cruise around the bay (▷ 75), visiting tiny beaches and islands. For more adventurous pursuits, head inland up the historic Estrada Real—the Gold Trail. The river here gushes over massive boulders. You can hike through jungle or zip from tree to tree in a high-wire adventure (▷ 75).

THE BASICS

www.pmparaty.rj.gov.br
∰ Map, ▷ 110
🛈 Avenida Roberto Silveira 1, tel (24) 3371 1222; daily 9–9
🚌 4 hours from Rio (Rodoviário Novo Rio, tel 3213 1800)

HIGHLIGHTS

- Pico da Tijuca
- Vista Chinesa
- Mirante Dona Marta
- Mesa do Imperador
- Pedra Bonita
- Waterfalls
- Wildlife
- Museu do Açude

TIP

● The park is vast and walking alone is not advisable. Outdoor adventure companies organize group hikes, including:
Curumim Eco Cultural Tours: tel 2217 7199, www.curumim.tur.br;
Florestaventura:
tel 2556 9462,
www.florestaventura.com;
Rio Hiking: tel 2552 9204,
www.riohiking.com.br;
Trilhas do Rio:
tel 2424 5455,
www.trilhasdorio.com.br.

This magnificent national park embraces Rio with lush forest; its trails offer superb walks and some of the best views in the city. Tijuca incorporates Rio's highest peaks and is one of the largest urban national parks in the world.

Man-made park It's hard to believe it now, looking at the dense green mountainsides, but much of the Tijuca National Park was re-planted in the 19th century. The fertile land was cleared in the 17th and 18th centuries to make way for sugar and coffee plantations. It was only following disastrous landslides that the authorities decided to restore the original landscape, launching a massive reforestation campaign between 1861 and 1888, planting more than 130,000 seedlings.

Clockwise from far left: The Pedra da Gávea; descending from the summit of Pico da Tijuca; the Cascatinha Taunay is one of many waterfalls in the area; looking out across the park from the top of Sugarloaf mountain

Exploring Tijuca today Tijuca became a national park in 1961, and dozens of trails now lead through the undergrowth and up to its peaks, such as Pico da Tijuca, at 1,022m (3,353ft), the tallest in Rio. The park covers an area from Santa Teresa to Jardim Botânico, including mountains such as Corcovado, Pedra da Gávea and Pedra Bonita. You can spend a whole day exploring the hillsides, coming across sparkling waterfalls and ponds and, if you're lucky, spotting toucans, blue morpho butterflies and monkeys. The park also has lookout points, such as the Vista Chinesa, Mesa do Imperador and Mirante Dona Marta, as well as the elegant Os Esquilos restaurant (▷ 146) and historic buildings such as the Capela Mayrink, Museu do Açude and the Fonte Wallace.

THE BASICS

www.amigosdoparque.org.br

⊞ A8

✉ Main entrance and ticket office: Praça Afonso Vizeu, Alto da Boa Vista, tel 2492 2252; daily 8–7

🍴 Os Esquilos ($$$) (▷ 146)

🚌 225, 233, 234 go to the main entrance from Saens Pena Metrô (Tijuca district)

♿ None

💲 Free

❓ The easiest way to arrive is by taxi or car

- Museu Imperial
- Palácio de Cristal
- Museu Casa de Santos Dumont
- Catedral de São Pedro de Alcântara
- Palácio Quitandinha
- Itatiaia National Park
- Serra dos Orgãos National Park

TIP

- Although a day trip is possible, Petrópolis deserves an overnight stay.

Former summer home of the Portuguese Royal Family, this town brims with historical architecture. With its cooler mountain air, it's a popular weekend destination for *cariocas*.

Royal retreat Emperor Dom Pedro I discovered this area nestled in the hillsides about an hour and a half from Rio, with a comfortably temperate climate. His son Pedro II developed Petrópolis as a summer retreat for the Royal Family, building the Imperial Palace, which has been immaculately preserved as a museum of Brazil's Imperial past.

Architecture The historical centre has handsome 19th-century mansions. German engineer Julio Frederico Koeler designed many of the finest buildings, and also planned

Clockwise from bottom left: the Catedral de São Pedro de Alcântara, dwarfed by the forest-clad slope rising behind it; Avenida Koeler; the cathedral contains the tombs of the Portuguese Royal Family; Palacio Rio Negro, one of the summer residences of the Brazilian president

the city layout, with tree-lined avenues flanking canalized rivers. Key buildings are the Catedral de São Pedro de Alcântara, with the Portuguese Royal Family tombs; the Palácio de Cristal, now used for flower shows and exhibitions; the Casa de Santos Dumont, eccentric home of the pioneer aviator; and the Palácio Quitandinha, former casino and showhall.

Walking up an appetite The surrounding countryside is known as the Valley of the Gourmets because of its high-quality restaurants. The fertile area has attracted an influx of immigrants, from Mexico to Japan, bringing with them cuisine from around the world. The area has some great hiking and climbing opportunities, with many parks, including the Serra dos Orgãos and Itatiaia national parks (▷ 74).

THE BASICS

www.pcvb.com.br
➕ Map, ▷ 111
ℹ️ Shopping Pinna Plaza, Estrada União e Indústria 10.510, Itaipava, Petrópolis, tel 0800 024 1516; Tue–Sun 10–6
🚌 1.5 hours from Rio (Rodoviário Novo Rio, tel 3213 1800)
❓ Food festivals include the German *Bauernfest* in Jun and *Petrópolis Gourmet* week in Nov

Imperial Palace and Museum

www.museuimperial.gov.br
✉️ Rua da Imperatriz 220
☎️ (24) 2245 5550
🕐 Tue–Sun 11–6
🍴 Restaurant/café ($$)
♿ Good
👎 Moderate
❓ Audioguide (R$3)

21 ⭐ Praça XV de Novembro

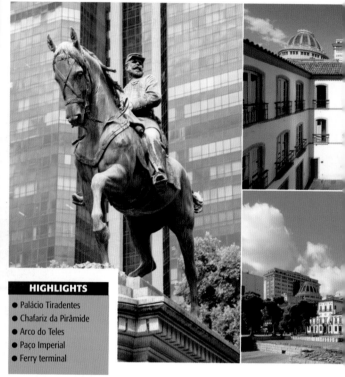

HIGHLIGHTS

- Palácio Tiradentes
- Chafariz da Pirâmide
- Arco do Teles
- Paço Imperial
- Ferry terminal

TIPS

- Thursday to Saturday Praça XV comes alive with street markets: on Thursday and Friday (8–6) you can buy food, crafts, clothes and curios; on Saturday it's antiques.
- Boats from the ferry terminal go to Niterói, Ilha de Paquetá and Ilha Grande (www.barcas-sa.com.br), as well as on cruises around the bay (Pink Fleet Cruises: www.pinkfleet.com.br).

This square is the ceremonial hub of downtown Rio and scene of key political events in Brazilian history.

Influential past Bordered by both modern and colonial buildings and, to the east, by the ferry terminal (Estaçao de Barcas), the Praça XV de Novembro was originally the site of a Carmelite convent, built in 1590. Warehouses were constructed here in the early 18th century and the Governor's palace, the Paço Imperial, in 1743. The square witnessed the coronations of Dom Pedro I and II, the abolition of slavery in 1888, and in 1889 the removal of Emperor Dom Pedro II. Today, several historic buildings have survived among the towering modern blocks and the square provides a welcome airy space.

Clockwise from far left: An equestrian statue of Marechel Osório; the Paço Imperial dates from the mid-18th century; an ornate lamp post; the Chafariz da Pirâmide fountain no longer has water flowing through it

Prominent features One of Praça XV's most iconic monuments is the Chafariz da Pirâmide, a fountain constructed in 1789. This once supplied ships with fresh water, although water no longer flows from the squat, pyramid-topped monument, as it was eroding the stone. The Paço Imperial, on its south side, is open to the public, with a range of permanent and temporary art exhibitions. Behind that is the Palácio Tiradentes, built on the site where the eponymous independence hero was imprisoned in 1792, and which is now the seat of the State Legislative Assembly.

Through the arch Opposite the Paço Imperial is the Arco do Teles, an archway leading to cobbled alleyways lined with rows of colonial houses. Some are now cafés, bars and shops.

THE BASICS

Praça XV de Novembro
+ G2
Ⓜ Carioca/Uruguaiana
🚌 123, 132

Paço Imperial
www.pacoimperial.com.br
✉ Largo do Paço, Praça XV
☎ 2533 4407
🕐 Tue–Sun 12–6
🍴 Restaurant ($$)
♿ Few
🎟 Free

Palácio Tiradentes
✉ Rua Primeiro de Março
☎ 2588 1411
🕐 Mon–Sat 10–5, Sun 12–5
♿ Few
🎟 Free

● The currents on Praia de São Conrado can be dangerous and the sea is not safe for swimmers. *Postos* (lifeguard stations) are every few hundred metres, signalled by a white flag with a red cross. A red flag means no one should enter the water.

● Rocinha, Rio's largest *favela* (▷ 73), borders São Conrado, and the locals also come to the beach. Most are friendly but they can get a bit boisterous.

Between Gávea and Barra da Tijuca, São Conrado has one of the city's best surfing beaches. It also has the lush Tijuca Forest as its jungle backdrop and hang-gliders land on its soft sands.

Fazenda farmland Today, São Conrado is a stylish modern suburb, with lawned and fenced condominiums and some of the city's smartest shopping centres, notably the giant Fashion Mall (▷ 121). The area was previously farmland, with sugar and coffee plantations operating until the early 20th century. Little of its historical architecture remains, however, except the Igreja de São Conrado (1916). The small church, which gave the area its name, stands between the main coastal highway and the Gávea Golf and Country Club. One plantation that

Praia de São Conrado is popular with surfers, hang-gliding enthusiasts and those who just want a quick game of bat-and-ball on the sands. Its tower blocks are bordered by Rocinha (top middle), Rio's largest favela

has survived now houses Villa Riso art gallery and restaurant, serving *feijoada* in a sumptuous setting, with live music.

Extreme activities São Conrado is a hot spot for outdoor adventure, with opportunities for surfing, bodyboarding, hang-gliding, paragliding, hiking and rock-climbing. Experienced surfers rate Praia de São Conrado highly, but it is not safe for swimmers, with powerful rip tides and undertow. The sea is usually polluted, especially after heavy rains. Praia Pepino, at the far end, is the most popular stretch for bodyboarders. Flat-topped Pedra da Gávea is a popular and challenging peak for rock climbers. Pedra Bonita, in the Tijuca National Park, has a take-off platform for hang-gliding over the treetops and landing on the soft sands of Praia Pepino.

THE BASICS

+ Map, ▷ 105 e4
† Beach snack bars ($)
🚌 175, 177, 523
♿ Few
❓ Local clubs organize climbs of Pedra da Gávea: Contact Trilhas do Rio (www.trilhasdorio.com.br). For tandem hang-gliding flights contact the Brazilian Hang-gliders Association (www.abvl.com.br)

Villa Riso
✉ Estrada da Gávea 728
☎ 3322 1444
🕐 Sun lunch only, from 1pm
🍽 Sun lunch expensive. No charge for gallery, but it is open only to diners
❓ Reserve ahead

23 Santa Teresa

HIGHLIGHTS

- *Bonde* (tram)
- Largo dos Guimarães
- Museu da Chácara do Céu
- Santa Teresa Cinema
- Views of city centre
- Art galleries
- Historic architecture

DID YOU KNOW?

- Santa Teresa's trams are called *bonde* because the original tickets looked like government bonds. The open-sided trams are still the cheapest form of transport in Rio (one-way tickets cost around R$0.55).

Rickety old trams rattle up to Santa Teresa, an area favoured by artists, but with a more refined air than Lapa below. The district is a magnet for visitors, offering museums, galleries and restaurants with superb views.

Wealthy origins The leafy hillsides of Santa Teresa formed the city's first wealthy neighbourhood, offering a cooler and healthier climate than the mosquito-infested coast. Spreading around the 17th-century convent, which gave the area its name, fine colonial mansions were built and Santa Teresa thrived until improvements in hygiene and infrastructure made the city centre more habitable.

Today The steep, cobblestoned streets are still lined with impressive old houses, some looking

Clockwise from far left: One of Santa Teresa's elegant colonial mansions; the Convento de Santa Teresa; travelling up the hill on the tram is a true Rio experience; colourful buildings; the eye-catching Escadaria Selarón steps lead from Lapa to Santa Teresa

a little age-worn now, but brimming with character and style. Many of Brazil's leading artists live and have galleries here. It is generally a safe place to explore, but it is bordered by more risky *favelas*, so don't wander alone down backstreets, especially at night.

Social hub The Largo dos Guimarães is a major junction, where the two tramlines split. It's also a social hub; there's an information desk in the police station, the beloved little Cine Santa Teresa (▷ 133), a bookshop and several cafés and restaurants. Just off the square is the tiny Museu do Bonde, a tram museum and workshop, and further uphill is the Museu da Chácara do Céu (▷ 70), the best museum and art gallery in the neighbourhood, worth the climb for the views alone.

THE BASICS

➕ E4

ℹ Information desk in the police station, on the corner of Largo dos Guimarães and Rua Paschoal Carlos Magno; open 24 hours

🚌 407 leaves from Largo do Machado. The tram from Lapa (Carioca) stops at Largo dos Guimarães

- Rare orchids
- Lily ponds
- 17th-century chapel
- Primitive ceramics
- Tropical gardens
- Burle Marx paintings and sculptures
- Plantation house

DID YOU KNOW?

- Mass takes place in the 17th-century Santo Antonio chapel every Sunday.
- On 13 June Guaratiba residents lead a procession up to the small chapel, ending in the coronation of the Holy Mary.

The home of Brazil's leading 20th-century landscape designer has beautiful grounds with tree-lined paths, lily ponds, bubbling streams, sculptures and mosaics. With 3,500 plant species, this is one of the world's most important botanical collections.

Inspired by Berlin Roberto Burle Marx (1909–94) was responsible for many of Rio's best-known urban landscapes, including Copacabana's mosaic esplanade and the Parque do Flamengo. He was first inspired by his native flora as a teenager, not by travelling around Brazil itself but during a two-year family trip to Europe. He visited the Dahlem Botanical Gardens in Berlin, with its display of Brazilian plants, and decided he would make his own collection. In 1949 Burle Marx bought a former

Clockwise from far left: Burle Marx's bedroom has been preserved as he left it; part of the indigenous ceramics collection; a piano graces one of the rooms; the tranquil gardens contain 3,500 plant species

banana plantation, between Grumari and Guaratiba. He restored the colonial buildings and cleared the grounds for the plants he had collected since he was six years old. He lived here from 1973 until his death.

Art and nature in harmony Guided tours include the gardens, the 17th-century chapel and the original plantation house, where Burle Marx lived, with his impressive collection of art and furniture. The house has been faithfully preserved, including Burle Marx's bedroom, his reading glasses still on the bedside table. The artworks include Burle Marx's own paintings, as well as pre-Colombian ceramics, religious icons and modern sculpture. Among the highlights is a collection of primitive pottery from the Vale da Jequitinhonha in Minas Gerais.

THE BASICS

➕ Map, ▷ 104 a4
✉ Estrada da Barra de Guaratiba 2019
☎ 2410 1412
🕐 Visits by pre-booked guided tours only, Tue–Sun 9.30, 1.30
🍽 None
🚌 867 from Copacabana
♿ Few
💲 Inexpensive
❓ Tours last 1.5 hours. Small gift shop, with toilets and drinking fountain

25 Vale do Café

- Coffee *fazendas*
- *Seresta* serenades
- Centímetro cinema

DID YOU KNOW?

- Cinephile Ivo Raposo runs Conservatória's tiny Centímetro cinema club (Rua Jose Ferreira Borges 205, Conservatória; irregular opening hours, weekend evenings), which he has decorated with art deco fittings salvaged from MGM cinemas in Rio.

The green hills of Rio's hinterland were once the heart of Brazil's coffee industry. Now, former *fazendas* (plantations) in the Coffee Valley have turned to tourism.

Coffee boom The Vale do Café lies in the valley of the Rio Paraíba do Sul, near Minas Gerais. Looking over the fertile pastures are historic plantation houses, survivors of the area's coffee-boom era. From 1825 to 1870 the region contributed 65 per cent of Brazil's coffee exports.

Fazenda tours More than 20 *fazendas* have opened their doors to visitors. Many are still family homes, with working farms and ranches, and are in stunning grounds. Some give guided tours, and some even perform

Clockwise from far left: A waterwheel sits on the side of the Pousada Fazenda de Ponte Alta; two palms stand guard in front of the plantation house; Vassouras is one of the main towns in the Vale do Café; an old coffee grinder; looking across the lawn to the Pousada Fazenda de Ponte Alta

re-enactments of life in the times of colonial masters and their slaves. Others simply offer a relaxing retreat. Fazenda da Taquara is the only coffee plantation still in production. The small estate, to the west of Vassouras, dates from 1815, with the sixth generation of the same family running the business today. Other outstanding *fazendas* are Paraíso, Vista Alegre, Cachoeira Grande, Ponte Alta and Florença.

Strolling minstrels The region's main towns of Valença, Vassouras and Conservatória are worth visiting for their architecture and lively cultural activities. Musicians in Conservatória have revived a popular tradition of *serestas* (serenades), with guitar-playing groups strolling the streets on weekend evenings and Sunday lunchtimes, singing romantic ballads.

THE BASICS

www.preservale.com.br

⊞ Map, ▷ 110

ℹ For details of all the *fazendas* open to visitors in the Vale do Café, and guided tours available, contact Preservale (see website above)

❓ Several of the *fazendas* sell home-made produce; these include Fazenda Vista Alegre, with bottled jams and preserves, and Fazenda Cachoeira Grande, which sells honey and other deli produce

More to See

This section contains other great places to visit if you have more time. Some are in the heart of the city while others are several hours' journey away, found under Further Afield. This chapter also has a fantastic excursion that you should set aside a whole day for.

In the Heart of the City

BARRA DA TIJUCA

With its 18km (11-mile) strip of white sand, Barra da Tijuca has the longest beach in Rio. The rapidly developing neighbourhood is also one of the city's most Americanized areas, with the highest number of shopping malls, bowling alleys and mega-sized nightclubs. Praia do Pepê (between *posto* 1 and *posto* 2) is one of the most popular areas of the beach for the young and wealthy. Here you'll find volleyball and football pitches, surfing and a lively nightlife scene. Media giant Globo has its main TV studios in Barra. Behind Barra are a number of lakes and green areas, including Bosque da Barra.

Map, ▷ 105 d4 ✉ Barra da Tijuca
🚍 175, 179, 523

CATEDRAL METROPOLITANA

www.catedral.com.br

Strikingly futuristic, the design of Rio's modern cathedral is based on a Maya pyramid. Inside the flat-topped conical building, glowing stained-glass panels relieve the bare expanses of concrete. Standing 96m (315ft) high and 106m (348ft) in diameter at its base, the cathedral was designed by architect Edgar Fonseca and completed in 1976. You can visit a sacred art museum in the cathedral's basement.

✚ F3 ✉ Avenida República do Chile 245, Centro ☎ 2240 2669 🕐 Daily 7–6. Museum: Wed 9–12, 1–4, Sat–Sun 9–12
🚇 Carioca ♿ Few 🎟 Free

CENTRO CULTURAL BANCO DO BRASIL

www.bb.com.br/cultura

This classical-style 19th-century building was converted in 1989 into a prominent cultural centre. With six floors containing two theatres, cinemas, exhibition space, a library, restaurant, café and bookshop, there's plenty to occupy your time here.

✚ G2 ✉ Rua Primeiro de Março 66, Centro ☎ 3808 2020 🕐 Tue–Sun 10–9
🍴 Restaurant ($$) and café ($)
🚇 Uruguaiana ♿ Good 🎟 Museum and exhibitions free; shows and cinema inexpensive

The beach at Barra da Tijuca

Catedral Metropolitana

CENTRO CULTURAL PARQUE DAS RUÍNAS

See the remains of the former home of belle époque socialite Laurinda Santos Lobo (1878–1946), now being restored and holding occasional exhibitions and concerts. The platforms and stairs offer great views over the city.

🔲 F4 ✉ Rua Murtinho Nobre 169, Santa Teresa ☎ 2252 1039 ⏰ Tue–Sun 10–8 🚌 206, 214. Tram to Largo do Curvelo ♿ Few 💲 Free

CIDADE DO SAMBA

http://cidadedosambarj.globo.com
This vast new exhibition centre, workshop and samba show hall in a revived dockside area displays Carnaval floats, costumes and memorabilia. There is also a samba show every Thursday.

🔲 E1 ✉ Rua Rivadavia Correia 60, Gamboa ☎ 2213 2503 ⏰ Tue–Sat 10–5 🍴 Café ($) 🚕 Take a taxi from Rodoviário Novo Rio bus terminal ♿ Few 💲 Inexpensive (Thu samba show and dinner expensive) ❓ Temporarily closed in 2011 due to a fire; check opening hours before visiting

ESCADARIA SELARÓN

http://selaron.net
Eccentric Chilean artist Jorge Selarón has transformed a flight of steps leading from Lapa up to Santa Teresa into a quirky artwork. He has covered each of the 215 steps with recycled ceramic tiles, creating a mosaic in blue, yellow and green—the colours of the national flag—as his tribute to Brazil. Selarón, who runs a small gallery near the bottom of the steps, is continuing the work he began in 1990, adding a fun splash of colour to his neighbourhood.

🔲 F4 ✉ Rua Joaquim Silva Lapa (behind Sala Cecília Meireles), Lapa ⏰ Daily 24 hours 🚇 Cinelândia 💲 Free

FEIRA DE SÃO CRISTÓVÃO

www.feiradesaocristovao.org.br
An enormous market dedicated to the rich culture of northeastern Brazil, the Feira de São Cristóvão has hundreds of stalls selling food, clothing, music, books and handicrafts. There's also live music and dance non-stop from

Inside the Centro Cultural Banco do Brasil

A labour of love – the Escadaria Selarón

Friday morning to Sunday night.
✠ B1 ⊠ Campo de São Cristóvão, São Cristóvão ☎ 2580 5335 ④ Tue–Thu 10–6, Fri 10am non-stop through to Sun 8pm 🍴 Restaurants and cafés ($–$$) 🚇 São Cristóvão 🚌 277 from Praça XV ♿ Few 🎫 Free

FORTE DE COPACABANA

www.fortedecopacabana.com
Strategically sited at the western end of Copacabana beach, this old fort offers great views across the bay and around Arpoador headland to Praia do Diabo. It has a branch of the coffee shop Confeiteria Colombo, a military museum and art exhibitions.
✠ E12 ⊠ Praça Coronel Eugenio Franco 1, Copacabana ☎ 2521 1032 ④ Tue–Sun 10–6 🍴 Restaurant ($$) 🚇 Cantagalo ♿ Few 🎫 Inexpensive

FUNDAÇÃO EVA KLABIN

www.evaklabin.org.br
The elegant home of Eva Klabin (1903–91), daughter of wealthy Lithuanian immigrants, contains her priceless collection of art treasures spanning 30 centuries.

This includes Renaissance icons, Impressionist landscape paintings and ancient ceramics. Tour guides tell of the owner's celebrated socialite lifestyle, with her lavish wardrobe lovingly displayed.
✠ D11 ⊠ Avenida Epitácio Pessoa 2480, Lagoa ☎ 3202 8550 ④ Guided tours by appointment only, Tue–Fri 2.30, 4 🚇 Cantagalo ♿ Few 🎫 Inexpensive

IGREJA E CONVENTO DE SANTO ANTÔNIO

Santo Antônio is the oldest church in Rio and is part of a 400-year-old architectural complex including a Franciscan monastery. Highlights include the richly decorated baroque chapel and a magnificent sacristy.
✠ F3 ⊠ Largo da Carioca, Centro ☎ 2262 0129 ④ Mon, Wed–Fri 7.30–7, Tue 6.30am–8pm, Sat 7.30–11, 3.30–5, Sun 9–11 🚇 Carioca; then lift up to church ♿ Few 🎫 Free

INSTITUTO MOREIRA SALLES

www.ims.com.br
This cool, white modernist building shelters an important collection of

Vivid-blue shutters on a building on Largo do Boticário

Forte de Copacabana

modern Brazilian art. The inner courtyard and mural were designed by Burle Marx (▷ 60).

➕ Map, ▷ 105 e4 ✉ Rua Marquês de São Vicente, Gávea ☎ 3284 7400 🕐 Tue–Sun 1–8 🍴 Café ($) 🚍 170, 504, 583, 592, 593 ♿ Few 🎟 Free

LARGO DO BOTICÁRIO

A picturesque little square in Cosme Velho, near the station for the Corcovado Train, the Largo do Boticário is lined by prettily painted colonial-style mansions. Some of these were salvaged from original buildings demolished in 1831 to make way for Avenida Presidente Vargas, one of downtown's major arteries. The square featured in the 1979 James Bond film *Moonraker*.

➕ D6 ✉ Rua Cosme Velho 822, Cosme Velho 🚆 Cosme Velho ♿ Easy access to square 🎟 Free

MONUMENTO NACIONAL AOS MORTOS DA SEGUNDA GUERRA MUNDIAL

www.mnmsgm.ensino.eb.br
Twin columns representing up-stretched arms form the focal point of the World War II Memorial, built in 1960 and designed by Hélio Marinho and Marcos Netto. Soldiers watch over the Tomb to the Unknown Soldier. There is an adjacent military museum.

➕ G4 ✉ Avenida Infante Dom Henrique, Aterro do Flamengo, Glória ☎ 2240 1283 🕐 Tue–Sun 10–4. Museum: daily 9–5 🚇 Glória ♿ Few 🎟 Free

MUSEU CARMEN MIRANDA

http://carmen.miranda.nom.br
A squat concrete building on Flamengo seafront, this little museum is nevertheless worth a visit for its memorabilia of Rio's first Hollywood diva, including her jewellery, costumes, turbans and shoes. It is due to close some time in 2012 and the collection will move to the new Museu da Imagem e da Som (Museum of Image and Sound), on Avenida Atlântica.

➕ G7 ✉ Parque do Flamengo (opposite Avenida Rui Barbosa 560), Flamengo ☎ 2334 4293 🕐 Tue–Fri 10–5, Sat 1–5 🚇 Flamengo ♿ Few 🎟 Free

The café in the Instituto Moreira Salles

The World War II Memorial

MUSEU DA CHÁCARA DO CÉU

www.museuscastromaya.com.br

This exquisite little museum was the home of art collector Raymundo Ottoni de Castro Maya (1894–1968) and is in a light and airy 1950s house next to the Centro Cultural Parque das Ruinas. Arranged over two floors, the collection includes antique furniture, ornaments and works by European and Brazilian artists, such as Portinari, Di Cavalcanti, Modigliani, Matisse and Picasso. The delightful garden is decorated with sculptures and shady seats, with spectacular views through the trees.

✚ F4 ⊠ Rua Murtinho Nobre 93, Santa Teresa ☎ 3970 1126 ◉ Wed–Mon 12–5 🚌 206, 214. Tram to Largo do Curvelo ♿ Few 🎟 Inexpensive (free Thu)

MUSEU DE FOLCLORE EDISON CARNEIRO

www.cnfcp.gov.br

This museum has a charming collection of Brazilian folk art, including wooden sculpture and ceramic figurines. The items are arranged in five themes, covering life, technology, religion, art and festivities.

✚ G5 ⊠ Rua do Catete 179, Catete ☎ 2285 0441 ◉ Tue–Fri 11–6, Sat–Sun 3–6 🚇 Catete ♿ Few 🎟 Free

MUSEU HISTÓRICO NACIONAL

www.museuhistoriconacional.com.br

One of Brazil's most important historical museums is housed in the 17th-century Forte de Santiago. Its huge collection comprises nearly 350,000 exhibits, including the largest display of coins in Latin America.

✚ H3 ⊠ Praça Marechal Ancora, Centro ☎ 2550 9224 ◉ Tue–Fri 10–5.30, Sat–Sun 2–6 🍴 Café ($) 🚇 Carioca ♿ Few 🎟 Moderate

MUSEU INTERNACIONAL DE ARTE NAÏF

www.museunaif.com.br

Visit this museum to see one of the biggest collections of naïve-style art in the world. There are some 6,000 paintings from all over Brazil and around the world, dating from the 15th century to

Outside the Museu Histórico Nacional

the present. The museum is housed in a 19th-century mansion set in grounds just next to the Corcovado station; it stages temporary exhibitions, workshops and courses.

If you're waiting for a train to Corcovado on a rainy day and have bored youngsters in tow, it's worth remembering that the museum is just a few minutes' walk away and has two huge, colourful artworks that should keep them amused: an enormous aerial view of Rio, depicting the city's famous landmarks; and a mural of Brazil's most important historical events and characters.

🔲 D7 ⊠ Rua Cosme Velho 561, Cosme Velho ☎ 2205 8612 🕐 Mon–Fri 1–5 🍴 Café ($) 🚇 Cosme Velho 🚌 422, 583, 584 ♿ Few 🎟 Inexpensive

NOSSA SENHORA DA CANDELÁRIA

One of Rio's most striking churches, Candelária looks out over the busy Praça Pio X. The neoclassical building, with twin bell towers, was completed in 1877,

its limestone dome transported from Portugal. The cool marble interior (▷ 64, picture) is lit up by stunning stained-glass windows.

🔲 G2 ⊠ Praça Pio X, Centro ☎ 2233 2324 🕐 Mon–Fri 7.30–4, Sat 8–12, Sun 9–1 🚇 Uruguaiana ♿ Few 🎟 Free

PALÁCIO DO CATETE

www.museudarepublica.org.br
This magnificent 19th-century mansion, a former seat of government, now houses the Museu da República, with an important collection of historical art and artefacts, including the room where, on 24 August 1954, President Getúlio Vargas committed suicide.

🔲 G5 ⊠ Rua do Catete 153, Catete ☎ 3235 3693 🕐 Tue–Fri 10–5, Sat–Sun 2–6 🍴 Cafeteria ($) 🚇 Catete ♿ Few 🎟 Inexpensive (free Wed, Sun)

PALÁCIO DAS LARANJEIRAS

In landscaped gardens in a quiet backstreet, this early 20th-century mansion is today the residence of the state governor of Rio. Guided tours show visitors the grand

The Salão de Banquetes in the Palácio do Catete

salons, which are decorated with period furniture and artwork. The grounds—Parque Guinle—have a small lake, paths and lawns, which are open to the public. Famous visitors to the Palácio das Laranjeiras have included former French president Charles de Gaulle and US president Harry Truman.

➕ F6 ✉ Rua Paulo Cesar de Andrade 407, Catete ☎ 2299 5233 🕐 Guided tours of the palace by appointment Tue, Thu 2, 3 🚌 406A, 422, 498, 583 ♿ Few ♿ Free

PARQUE DA CIDADE

www.aamcrj.org

Once a coffee plantation, this park now has forest trails, waterfalls, ponds and a playground. A 19th-century mansion houses the Museu da Cidade, with art, furniture and items relating the history of Rio de Janeiro up to the 1930s.

➕ Map, ▷ 105 e4 ✉ Estrada de Santa Marinha 505, Gávea ☎ 2274 0096/ 2512 2353 🕐 Park: daily 8–5. Museum: Tue–Fri 10–4, Sat–Sun 10–3 🚌 170, 504, 583, 592, 593 ♿ Few ♿ Free

PARQUE ECOLÓGICO CHICO MENDES

This marshland nature reserve is dedicated to Chico Mendes, an Amazonian environmental campaigner who was assassinated in 1988. Sandy pathways lead among the mangroves and cacti, which are home to many birds, butterflies and reptiles, including the endangered broad-nosed cayman. An observation tower looks over the Lagoinha dos Jacarés to the coastline beyond.

➕ Map, ▷ 104 b4 ✉ Avenida Jarbas de Carvalho 679, Recreio dos Bandeirantes ☎ 2437 6400 🕐 Mon–Fri 9–5.30 🍽 None 🚌 175, 179 ♿ Few ♿ Free

QUINTA DA BOA VISTA

www.museunacional.ufrj.br

The Imperial Palace, former home of the Portuguese Royal Family, now houses the Museu Nacional, a superb natural history museum. The surrounding park and landscaped grounds contain boating lakes and restaurants, as well as RIOZOO, a small zoo and aquarium with 2,000 animals,

Some of the 350,000 books housed in the Real Gabinete Português da Leitura

including many indigenous species.
🏠 B2 ✉ Quinta da Boa Vista, São Cristóvão
☎ 2562 6900 🕐 Park: daily 9–6. Museum:
Tue–Sun 10–4. Zoo: Tue–Sun 9–4.30
🍴 Restaurant ($$) and café ($) 🚇 São
Cristóvão ♿ Few 🎫 Inexpensive

REAL GABINETE PORTUGUÊS DA LEITURA

www.realgabinete.com.br
The magnificent Portuguese Royal
Library and Reading Room,
founded in 1837, contains some
350,000 books dating from the
16th century to the present,
including many rare leather-bound
volumes, shelved on three floors
of ornately carved galleries.
🏠 F2 ✉ Rua Luís de Camões 30, Centro
☎ 2221 3138 🕐 Mon–Fri 9–6
🚇 Uruguaiana ♿ Few 🎫 Free

ROCINHA

The biggest *favela*, or shanty town,
in Brazil, Rocinha covers the hill-
sides between São Conrado and
Gávea in a jumble of ramshackle
concrete blocks and steep alley-
ways, home to an estimated
150,000 inhabitants. Going there
on your own is not advisable, but
tours can be highly rewarding,
particularly those run by local resi-
dents. Favela Tours runs organized
visits to Rocinha and helps support
a school in Vila Canoas, a nearby
favela (contact Marcelo Armstrong,
tel 3322 2727; www.favelatour.
com.br). Alternatively, Zezinho,
who lives in Rocinha, runs Favela
Adventures, which takes tours of
the backstreets to meet his neigh-
bours. Zezinho, who is a DJ, also
organizes *baile funk* parties (tel
3717 2269; www.favelatour.org).
Rocinha is a tricky sprawl to get
into and out of, though there are
minibuses from various areas,
including Ipanema. Guided tour
operators will either tell you a
meeting point to take a taxi to
or will pick you up from your
hotel. Although most residents are
hardworking, law-abiding citizens,
there is a risk of pickpocketing in
Rocinha. However, for those inter-
ested, the tours are a good way of
seeing the 'other side' of Rio.
🏠 Map, ▷ 105 e4 ✉ Rocinha
🎫 Tours: inexpensive

Rocinha, Rio's biggest shanty town, is home to around 150,000 people

Further Afield

ANGRA DOS REIS

www.turisangra.com.br

This upmarket coastal resort lies on the Costa Verde, the gorgeous strip of greenery between Rio and Santos to the west. Cruise the bay to visit nearby beaches and islands, or ride an old steam locomotive, the Trem Verde, through the Atlantic Forest.

🗺 Map, ▷ 110 ⊠ 160km (100 miles) from Rio on BR-101 🚻 Avenida Ayrton Senna 580, Praia do Anil, tel (24) 3367 7826; daily 8–8 🚌 From Rio's main bus station

ILHA GRANDE

www.turisangra.com.br

Ilha Grande is the largest of some 360 tropical islands along the Costa Verde, its crumpled mountains covered with dense forest, and criss-crossed with trails leading to empty beaches.

🗺 Map, ▷ 110 ⊠ 160km (100 miles) from Rio on BR-101 to Angra dos Reis, then 1 hour by ferry to Abraão 🚻 Avenida Ayrton Senna 580, Praia do Anil, Angra dos Reis, tel (24) 3367 7826; daily 8–8 🚌 From Angra dos Reis to the island's port, Abraão 🚢 Cruises around the island leave from Angra dos Reis

PARQUE NACIONAL DO ITATIAIA

www4.icmbio.gov.br/parna_itatiaia

This area became Brazil's first national park in 1937. Pico das Agulhas Negras, with its dark, jagged crags, is the third-highest mountain in Brazil (2,787m/8,445ft).

🗺 Map, ▷ 110 ⊠ 167km (100 miles) from Rio via BR-116 🚻 Avenida Wanderbilt de Barros, 4.5km, Itatiaia, tel (24) 3352 1652; daily 8–5 (Visitor Centre and Natural History Museum) 🍴 Cafeteria ($) in Visitor Centre 🚌 To Itatiaia, then short taxi ride 🚻 Few 🅼 Moderate (park and museum)

PARQUE NACIONAL SERRA DOS ORGÃOS

www.icmbio.gov.br/parnaso

The fingerlike peaks of Dedo de Deus, visible from Rio de Janeiro, are contained within this mountainous national park between Petrópolis and Teresópolis.

🗺 Map, ▷ 110 ⊠ 87km (54 miles) from Rio on BR-040 and BR-116 🚻 Avenida Rotariana, Soberbo, tel (21) 2642 1070; daily 8–5 🍴 Cafeteria ($) 🚌 To Teresópolis, then short taxi ride 🚻 Few 🅼 Moderate

Sunset, seen from Ilha Grande

Dedo de Deus, in the Parque Nacional Serra dos Orgãos

Excursion

PARATY BAY CRUISE

Explore Paraty Bay by boat, discovering empty beaches and tropical islands. Traditional schooners take groups on day cruises, or you can paddle a sea kayak and get closer to nature, visiting shallow bays and inlets. Even on cloudy days the sun is powerful; bring high-factor sun block and plenty of water.

Paraty Bay is dotted with hundreds of pristine beaches and islands, many of which are accessible only by sea, with dense jungle running down to the shore. Cruises offer an opportunity to swim in the bay's crystal-clear waters and discover the area's stunning coastline. You'll also be rewarded with amazing views of the old town (▷ 49) from the sea, the white-washed church towers and tiled rooftops framed against the green wall of mountains looming behind.

Schooners moored at the jetty next to Paraty's fish market run day cruises around the bay. Cruises usually last from 11am to 4pm, stopping at two islands and two beaches (though some are private and can only be seen from the boat). The most popular destinations are Praia Vermelha, Praia de Lula, Ilha Comprida—ideal for young families, with calm seas great for snorkelling and lots of colourful fish—and, lastly, Ilha Mantimento, home to the extremely rare Golden Lion Tamarin, with only an estimated 2,000 left in the wild.

Some schooners have an on-board bar and restaurant, others stop for a picnic lunch on a beach. The cruises are great fun but they can be a bit raucous, with loud music and a party atmosphere. If you want to escape the crowds and soak up some tropical tranquillity, sea kayaks offer a quieter alternative. You'll have to use your own muscle power, of course, but you can visit smaller bays, inlets and mangroves, with a better chance of spotting exotic wildlife.

Time: Schooner Cruises: 5 hours.
Sea Kayak expeditions: 4 hours to 4 days.

Paraty Explorer
www.paratyexplorer.com
Coastal kayaking, rainforest hikes, mountain biking and jungle high-wire circuits.
➕ Map, ▷ 110
✉ Rua das Canelas 17, Portal Sul, Paraty
☎ (24) 9952 4496

Paraty Tours
www.paratytours.com.br
Largest travel company in Paraty, with schooner cruises and kayak tours.
➕ Map, ▷ 110
✉ Avenida Roberto Silveira 11, Paraty
☎ (24) 3371 2651

Tourist Information Office
www.pmparaty.rj.gov.br
➕ Map, ▷ 110
✉ Avenida Roberto Silveira, Paraty
☎ (24) 3371 2899

Boats moored near Santa Rita church

City Tours

This section contains self-guided tours that will help you explore the sights in each of the city's regions. Each tour is designed to take one or two days, with a map pinpointing the recommended places along the way. There is a quick reference guide at the end of each tour, listing everything you need in that region, so you know exactly what's close by.

CITY TOURS

Downtown and Northern Rio

This is Rio's historic heartland, with the former capital's Imperial palaces, squares and churches amid the modern office blocks. There are also some fine museums and galleries here, and you can discover atmospheric local bars down shady side streets.

Morning
Start your day on **Praça XV de Novembro** (▷ 54–55). Head through the Arco do Teles and wander the narrow alleys lined with cafés and shops, passing the **Centro Cultural Banco do Brasil** (▷ 66). Cross the busy Praça Pio X and take the elevator up to the **Mosteiro de São Bento** (▷ 34–35), a 17th-century Benedictine Monastery whose interior is emblazoned with gold leaf.

Mid-morning
Walk back down via the winding Rua Dom Gerardo and onto Avenida Rio Branco, one of the busiest arterial thoroughfares, lined with shops, cafés and offices. Take a short detour right down Rua do Ouvidor to the **Real Gabinete Português da Leitura** (▷ 73), the magnificent 19th-century Portuguese Royal Library.

Lunch
Just a few blocks from the library is one of Rio's most revered old coffee shops, the **Confeitaria Colombo** (▷ 146), tucked away on Rua Gonçalves Dias, a quiet side street. You can feast on a buffet lunch here, but most visitors swoon for the home-made cakes and pastries in its gleaming cabinets. The upstairs area is reserved for lunches, offering a wonderful view of the art nouveau interior.

Afternoon

With your batteries now re-charged, wander a few blocks south to **Cinelândia**, downtown's entertainment hub, and base for nearby museums, galleries and concert halls. The **Museu Nacional de Belas Artes** (▷ 42–43) is Rio's biggest art museum, housing thousands of paintings from around Brazil, as well as many European masterpieces.

Mid-afternoon

Have a break for a drink in one of the many local bars *(botecos)* dotted around Cinelândia—**Bar Luiz** (▷ 143) is one of the most traditional downtown favourites. Try a chilled *suco de açaí*—the energy-packed tropical fruit is a great pick-me-up.

Dinner

As daytime moves into evening, in the alleyways off the **Arco do Teles**, where you started your day, bars and cafés come alive with the night crowd spilling out onto the street and with music filling the air. Once you've worked up an appetite over a cocktail and a *petisco* (bar snack), head for **Albamar** (▷ 142), one of downtown's best fish and seafood restaurants, with a great view over Guanabara Bay.

Evening

The area around **Arcos da Lapa** (▷ 33) comes alive in the evening with commuters having a drink after work (weekdays) and partygoers gathering for a night out. The **Fundição Progresso** (▷ 134) and **Circo Voador** (▷ 133) are two music venues that attract a lively crowd.

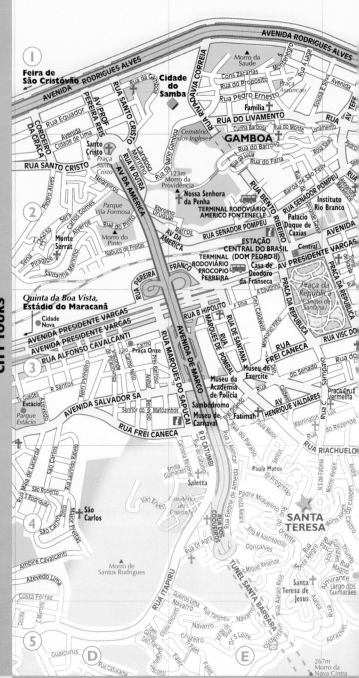

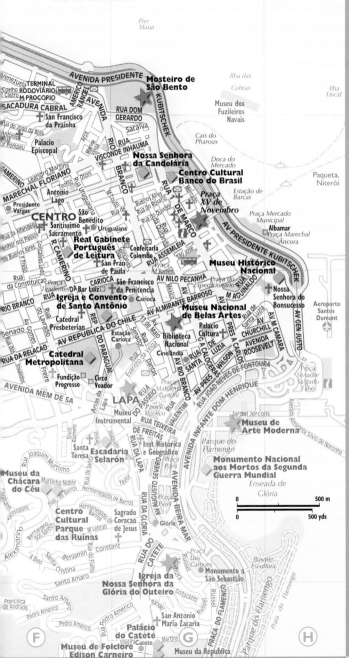

Baia de Guanabara

Pier Mauá

Ilha das Cobras

Ilha Fiscal

AVENIDA PRESIDENTE KUBITSCHEK

Mosteiro de São Bento

TERMINAL RODOVIÁRIO

Venezuela
Coelho Castro
M PROCOPIO
SACADURA CABRAL

AMERICO RANGEL AVENIDA

RUA DOM GERARDO

Museu dos Fuzileiros Navais

San Francisco da Prainha

Saraiva

RUA

Cais do Pharoux

Rua do Jogo da Bola

Palacio Episcopal

VISCONDE INHAUMA

RIO

Antonio Pompeu

Nossa Senhora da Candelária

Doca do Mercado

Paqueta, Niterói

MARECHAL FLORIANO

Leandro Martins

RUA URUGUAIANA

BRANCO

Centro Cultural Banco do Brasil

Estação de Barcas

Presidente Vargas

Antonio Lago

Buenos Aires

Praça XV de Novembro

Praça Mercado Municipal

CENTRO

São Benedito

Rua do Rosario

Rua do Ouvidor

RUA 1° DE MARÇO

Albamar

Santissimo Sacramento

Uruguaiana

Praça Marechal Âncora

Real Gabinete Português de Leitura

Confeitaria Colombo

San Fran-cisco de Paula

RUA ASSEMBLEIA

Museu Histórico Nacional

AV NILO PEÇANHA

Praça do Expedicionario

Rua da Constituicao

Praça Tiradentes

D A Bar Luiz

São Francisco da Penitencia

Carioca

Nossa Senhora do Bonsucesso

Aeroporto Santos Dumont

RUA CARIOCA

Igreja e Convento de Santo Antônio

AV ALMIRANTE BARROSO

M AQUINALDO

RIO BRANCO

Catedral Presbterian

REP DO PARAGUAI

AV REPUBLICA DO CHILE

Museu Nacional de Belas Artes

Santa Luzia

AV CHURCHILL

Senado

Estação Carioca

Palacio Cultura

AVENIDA

Catedral Metropolitana

13 DE MAIO

Biblioteca Nacional

ROOSEVELT

AVENIDA MEM DE SA

Fundição Progresso

Circo Voador

Cinelândia

RUA SANTA LUZIA

M CAMARA

AV PRES A CARLOS

Praça Senador Salgado Filho

LAPA

Museu Instrumental

RUA DO PASSEIO

Passeio Público

Praça Mahatma Gandhi

AV RIO BRANCO

RUA JOAO NEVES DE FONTOURA

Museu de Arte Moderna

RUA TEIXEIRA

DE FREITAS

Inst Histórica e Geográfico

AVENIDA INFANTE DOM HENRIQUE

Jardel Jercolis

Santa Teresa

Escadaria Selarón

RUA DA LAPA

Praça Paris

Parque do Flamengo

Museu da Chácara do Céu

Monumento Nacional aos Mortos da Segunda Guerra Mundial

Murtinho Nobre

Hermenegildo de Barros

AVENIDA BEIRA MAR

Enseada de Glória

Centro Cultural Parque das Ruínas

Sagrado Coração de Jesus

RUA DA GLORIA

0   500 m

0   500 yds

Glória

RUA DO CATETE

Igreja da Nossa Senhora da Glória do Outeiro

Praça Luis Camões

Monumento a São Sebastião

San Antonio Maria Zacaria

Pedro Americo

Palácio do Catete

PRAÇA DO FLAMENGO

Praia do Flamengo

Museu de Folclore Edison Carneiro

Museu da República

F   G   H

Downtown and Northern Rio
Quick Reference Guide

 SIGHTS AND EXPERIENCES

Estádio do Maracanã (▷ 22)

At Rio's vast football stadium, local derbies rival Carnaval for passionate exuberance. The legendary Pele scored his 1,000th goal here in 1969 and the Maracanã will stage football's World Cup Finals in 2014, when the contest comes to Brazil again.

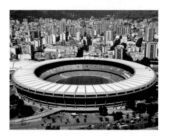

Mosteiro de São Bento (▷ 34)

The plain exterior of this 17th-century church on a city centre hillside hides a dazzling interior covered in gold leaf and brimming with historic artwork. Rio's rococo treasure, it's one of the most significant examples of religious architecture in the country.

Museu Nacional de Belas Artes (▷ 42)

The city's leading art museum includes European masterpieces, modernist Brazilian naïve paintings and African folk art. The initial collection of some 800 items has now grown to around 16,000 artworks.

Praça XV de Novembro (▷ 54)

Rio's most important colonial square is flanked by major colonial buildings in the heart of downtown, and has witnessed key historic events, including the coronations of two kings. Among its iconic monuments is the Chafariz da Pirâmide fountain.

CITY TOURS

82

MORE TO SEE 64

Catedral Metropolitana
Centro Cultural Banco do Brasil
Cidade do Samba
Feira de São Cristóvão
Igreja e Convento de Santo Antônio
Museu Histórico Nacional
Nossa Senhora da Candelária
Quinta da Boa Vista
Real Gabinete Português da Leitura

SHOP 114

Art and Handicrafts
O Equilibrista
Pé de Boi
Food, Drink and Markets
Saara (▷ 121, panel)

Shopping Malls
Vertical Shopping

ENTERTAINMENT 126

Cinemas and Theatres
Theatro Municipal
Clubs and Dancehalls
Circo Voador
Elite

Estudantina
The Week
Concert Halls
Fundição Progresso

EAT 138

Cafés and Bars
Armazém Senado
Bar Luiz
Bistro the Line
Confeitaria Colombo
Meat Feasts
Beduíno

Seafood
Albamar
Margutta Cittá
Vegetarian
Tempeh

Baia de Guanabara

The unrivalled star of Guanabara Bay is the Pão de Açúcar—
Sugarloaf—one of Rio's most famous sights. But Urca, the quiet
neighbourhood at the foot of the mountain, also has a blissfully
secluded beach, Praia Vermelha, and a delightful little nature trail.
Nearby Botafogo has one of Brazil's best museums dedicated to its
indigenous people, the Museu do Índio.

Morning
Make an early start to the day in
the cooler morning air, walking
the **Pista Claudio Coutinho**, a
paved trail of about 2.5km
(1.5 miles) around the foot of
Morro da Urca, the smaller peak
adjacent to Sugarloaf. On one side
the steep massif rises up through
lush forest fringe, on the other is
the bay and its rocky islets, both
giving spectacular views. The start
of the self-guided trail is marked
by a signpost at the far end of the
little beach, **Praia Vermelha**.
Information boards along the way
list commonly seen flora and
fauna such as capuchin monkeys,
which often come down from the
trees to feed on bananas left out
for them by appreciative locals.

Mid-morning
Return to Praia Vermelha and cool off in the calm waters of this
family-friendly beach.

Lunch
Praia Vermelha is flanked by
several good restaurants.
The **Praia Vermelha
Restaurante** (▷ 149), for
instance, operates the
popular self-service *por kilo*
system—pay by the weight
of your food—and is
excellent value for money.

Afternoon
Take a short taxi ride (from the square behind the beach) to the **Museu do Índio** (▷ 40–41), in a colonial mansion on a quiet residential backstreet in nearby Botafogo.

Mid-afternoon
Return to Praia Vermelha and hop on a cable car, which whisks you up to **Pão de Açúcar** (▷ 46–47) in a few breathtaking minutes. Soak up the amazing panorama from your rocky perch, 395m (1,296ft) above the sea, with views along the coast, fringed by the forest-clad peaks of **Tijuca National Park** (▷ 50–51), and across the bay to **Niterói** (▷ 44–45). Stay on Sugarloaf for sunset and you'll be rewarded with one of Rio's most stunning spectacles, as the city lights sparkle in the waves and the statue of **Cristo Redentor** (▷ 20–21) seems to float above Corcovado, illuminated on the horizon.

Dinner
There are a couple of glitzy but rather touristy restaurants on Pão de Açúcar and Morro da Urca, but for a special treat, jump in a taxi and go to **Porcão Rio's** (▷ 149), one of the city's most famous *churrascaria* restaurants—an eat-all-you-can meat feast in a superb setting in Parque Flamengo, with views across the Baia de Guanabara. End the day with a live gig at **Canecão** (▷ 133, panel), one of Rio's top concert halls, a short taxi ride away at the end of Botafogo Bay.

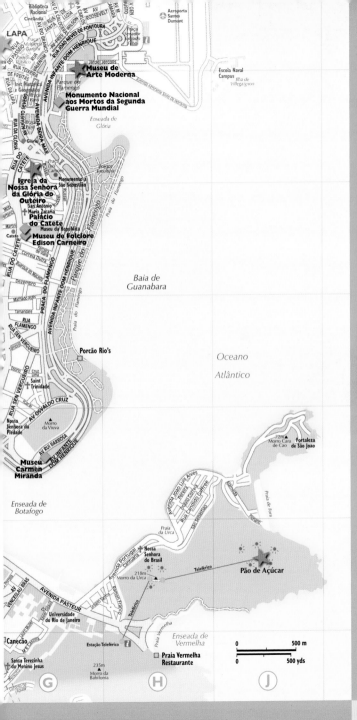

LAPA

Museu de Arte Moderna

Monumento Nacional aos Mortos da Segunda Guerra Mundial

Enseada de Glória

Biblioteca Nacional Cinelândia

Aeroporto Santos Dumont

Escola Naval Campus
Ilha de Villegaignon

Jardim Jercolis

Parque do Flamengo

Igreja da Nossa Senhora da Glória do Outeiro

San Antonio

Maria Zacana

Palácio do Catete

Museu da República

Museu de Folclore Edison Carneiro

Monumento a São Sebastião

Baia de Guanabara

Porcão Rio's

Saint Trinidade

Oceano Atlântico

Nossa Senhora da Piedade

Morro da Viuva

Museu Carmen Miranda

Enseada de Botafogo

72m Morro Cara de Cao

Fortaleza de São João

Praia de fora

Avenida João Luis Alves Pereira

Praia da Urca

Nossa Senhora do Brasil

218m Morro da Urca

Teleférico

Pão de Açúcar

AVENIDA PASTEUR

Universidade do Rio de Janeiro

Canecão

Santa Terezinha do Menino Jesus

Estação Teleférico

235m Morro da Babilonia

Praia Vermelha

Enseada de Vermelha

☐ **Praia Vermelha Restaurante**

0 — 500 m

0 — 500 yds

G   H   J

TOP 25 SIGHTS AND EXPERIENCES

Igreja da Nossa Senhora da Glória do Outeiro (▷ 24)

This pretty little 18th-century church has long been considered *cariocas'* favourite. Sitting on a hilltop by the Glória Marina, it dominates a lesser-known neighbourhood. Highlights inside include the *azulejos* (tiles).

Museu de Arte Moderna (▷ 36)

In a striking modern building in the Parque do Flamengo, Rio's modern art museum is largely comprised of a private collection. This was donated after a massive fire devastated most of the museum's original works in the early 1990s.

Museu do Índio (▷ 40)

One of the city's best specialist museums, the Museu do Índio is devoted to Brazil's long-suffering indigenous peoples. There are permanent and temporary exhibitions focusing on tribal culture, ritual and everyday life. Highlights include feathered head-dresses and sound recordings.

Pão de Açúcar Cable-Car Ride (▷ 46)

Hop up the twin peaks of Sugarloaf in a glass-walled cable car and see the sun set over the city. It's a breathtaking journey and an unforgettable experience, even if you do share it with some 2,000 others who take the trip every day. You may even spot monkeys.

MORE TO SEE 64

Monumento Nacional aos Mortos da Segunda Guerra Mundial
Museu Carmen Miranda
Museu de Folclore Edison Carneiro
Palácio do Catete

ENTERTAINMENT 126

Concert Venues
Canecão (▷ 133, panel)

Music Festivals
Verão do Morro

EAT 138

Brazilian
Lamas
Yorubá
European
Miam Miam

Meat Feasts
Porcão Rio's
Por Kilo Restaurants
Praia Vermelha Restaurante

The awe-inspiring view from Sugarloaf mountain

Copacabana, Ipanema and Leblon

Rio's most famous districts encapsulate *cariocas'* reputation for a fun-loving lifestyle, body toning and, yes, beach football. The beaches here buzz with life from dawn until dusk.

Morning

Start your walk at the far end of **Copacabana** beach (▷ 18–19), near the entrance to the **Forte de Copacabana** (▷ 68). There has been a fish market here for many years, and the fishermen sit in the cool shade under the trees, mending their nets or painting their traditional wooden boats. Take a stroll along the promenade, with its distinctive wavy black-and-white mosaic pavement. You'll pass the Museu da Imagem e da Som (Museum of Image and Sound), an ambitious new museum dedicated to music, the arts and cinema (due to open in 2012). Midway along the seafront you'll come to the majestic Copacabana Palace Hotel, the neighbourhood's grand old dame, with its classic facade.

Mid-morning

Drop in on the **Copacabana Palace Hotel** to see a photographic gallery of some of the world leaders and A-list celebs who have stayed here since its glamour days of the 1920s—from Noël Coward to Will Smith.

Back on the beach, relax at a seafront snack bar and have a refreshing *leite de coco*—coconut milk served straight from the shell.

Lunch

Cut across the headland dividing Copacabana and Ipanema, down Avenida Rainha Elisabete da Bélgica, and choose from one of the restaurants on Praça General Osório, a couple of blocks from the seafront. The **Casa da Feijoada** (▷ 145), on the corner with Rua Prudente de Morais, is named after Brazil's national dish, and is one of the best places to eat this rich meat stew, washed down with a shot of cachaça.

Afternoon

Have a break on Ipanema beach. In contrast to the bustle of neighbouring Copacabana, sophisticated **Ipanema** (▷ 26–27) has a more laidback pace. This is Rio's people-watching beach par excellence, with different groups concentrated around 'their' adopted *posto* (lifeguard station).

Mid-afternoon

Browse the chic boutiques and designer stores; and if you go on a Sunday, hunt for a bargain at the **Hippy Market**.

Early evening

Mingle with the local jet set for a cocktail at **Baretto Londra** (▷ 131), the rooftop bar at **Fasano** (▷ 156), Ipanema's coolest designer hotel. Or slum it with the masses on the beach, who raise a cool beer in tribute to the sun every night, as it sets between the dramatic silhouettes of Dois Irmãos and Pedra da Gávea.

Dinner

A short walk five blocks inland brings you to **Lagoa** (▷ 30–31), the upscale neighbourhood spread around Lagoa Rodrigo de Freitas. By night, the lagoon sparkles romantically, lit up by numerous waterside bars and restaurants. You can take your pick from cuisine from around the world, but a perennial favourite is the **Palaphita Kitch** (▷ 31), where you can sit under the stars and sample exotic Amazonian fish, such as *tucunaré* and the giant *pirarucu*. Round off your day strolling around the lakeshore, maybe having a nightcap in one of the other restaurants, some of which also have live music.

Morro da
Formiga

Rua Almirante Alexandrino

Itamonte
Indianna

Estrada do Sumaré

Estrada das Paineiras

Silvestre

Estrada Heitor da Silva

Estrada Miranda Dona Marta

Estrada Mirante Dona Marta

Estrada das Paineiras

539km

Estrada Redentor

Estrada da Redentor

Corcovado
Estação Monumento
do Corcovado
704m

Cristo Redentor

TÚNEL ANTÔNIO REBOUÇAS

TÚNEL ANDRÉ REBOUÇAS

*Parque
Nacional
da Tijuca*

Maria Eugênia

Morro do
Martelo

Alfredo Duarte

Instituto
Nacional de
Belas Artes

*Parque
Lage*

LAGOA

RUA JARDIM BOTÂNICO

AV LINEU DE RUA PAULA MACHADO

Divina
Providencia

São José
da Lagoa

AVENIDA
BORGES DE MEDEIROS

Parque Sacopenapa

RUA PROF A LOBO

AV EPITÁCIO PESSOA

RUA DA FONTE DA SAUDADE

Rua Pachaco Leão

BORGES DE MEDEIROS

Jardim Botânico

Museu-Sitio
Arqueológico
Casa dos Pilões

*Ilha
Piraque*

*Lagoa
Rodrigo de Freitas*

Museu
Carciologico

RUA JARDIM BOTÂNICO

*Parque
Tivoli*

Ponta de
Pires

AVENIDA
EPITÁCIO PESSOA

Joquei
Clube

Hipodromo
da Gávea

*Parque
Brig Farial
Lima*

Teatro
da Lagoa

Palaphita Kitch

*Parque
do
Cantagalo*

AV BARTOLOMEU MITRE

Estadio do
Remo do
Flamengo

*Ilha dos
Caicaras*

PADRE
FRANÇA

RUA
MÁRIO RIBEIRO

Clube de
Regatas
Flamengo

BORGES DE MEDEIROS

Cesar
Andrade

Russel

Rua Gilberto Cardoso

Clube
dos Caicaras

AVENIDA EPITÁCIO PESSOA

Saddock

AV AFRÂNIO DE MELO FRANCO

Rua Humberto de Campos

*Jardim
de Alalah*

Barão de Jaguaripe

Nascimento da Silva

Barão de Jaguaripe

Nascimento da Silva

Humberto de Campos

AV BARTOLOMEU MITRE

LEBLON

ATAULFO DE PAIVA

Santa
Mônica
San Martin

Prof A M

Redentor
Barão da Torre

Amsterdam
Sauer

IPANEMA

RUA VISCONDE DE PIRAJÁ

*Praça
Nossa
Senhora
da Paz*

RUA MARIA QUITÉRIA

Nossa
Senhora
da Paz

RUA VISCONDE DE PIRAJÁ

AV EPITÁCIO PESSOA

Barão da Torre

AVENIDA
DELFIM MOREIRA

Rua Prudente de Morais

AVENIDA
VIEIRA SOUTO

Rua Prudente de Morais

AVENIDA
VIEIRA SOUTO

Praia do Leblon

Praia do Leblon

Praia do Ipanema

Praia do Ipanema

A   B   C

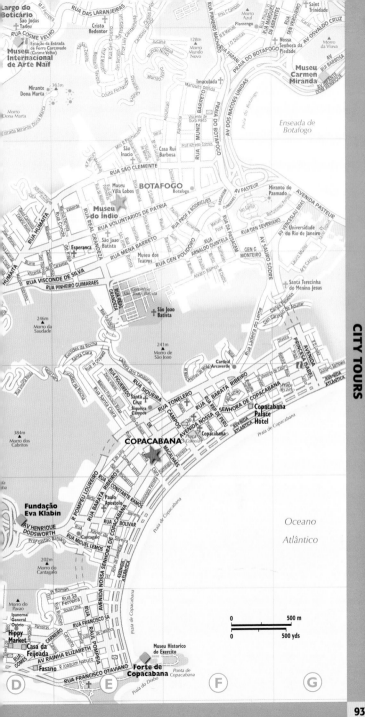

Largo do Boticário
São Judas Tadeu
RUA COSME VELHO
Cristo Redentor
Museu Internacional de Arte Naïf
Estação da Estrada de Ferro Corcovado (Cosme Velho)
Mirante Dona Marta 363m
Morro Dona Marta
Estrada Mirante Dona Marta

Museu Carmen Miranda

128m Morro Mundo Novo

Saint Trinidade
AV OSVALDO CRUZ
Morro Azul
Flamengo
Nossa Senhora da Piedade
Morro da Viúva

PRAIA DO BOTAFOGO
AV DAS NAÇÕES UNIDAS

Enseada de Botafogo

Imaculada
Marques Olinda

BOTAFOGO
Museu Villa Lobos
Botafogo

RUA SÃO CLEMENTE
São Inácio
Casa Rui Barbosa

Museu do Índio
RUA VOLUNTÁRIOS DE PATRIA
São João Batista
Esperança
Museu dos Teatros
RUA GEN POLIDORO

AV PASTEUR
Mirante do Pasmado
AVENIDA PASTEUR

Universidade do Rio de Janeiro

RUA VISCONDE DE SILVA
RUA PINHEIRO GUIMARÃES

Santa Terezinha do Menino Jesus

São João Batista

246m Morro da Saudade

241m Morro de São João

Cardeal Arcoverde

COPACABANA
Copacabana Palace Hotel
Praia de Copacabana

384m Morro dos Cabritos

RUA SIQUEIRA
Santa Cruz
RUA TONELERO
RUA BARATA RIBEIRO
AVENIDA NOSSA SENHORA DE COPACABANA
AVENIDA ATLÂNTICA

Paulo Apóstolo
RUA POMPEU LOUREIRO
RUA CONSTANTE RAMOS
RUA BOLIVAR

Fundação Eva Klabin
AV HENRIQUE DODSWORTH

202m Morro do Cantagalo

Oceano Atlântico

Morro do Pavão
Ipanema/General Osório
Hippy Market
Casa da Feijoada
Fasano
AV RAINHA ELIZABETH
RUA FRANCISCO OTAVIANO

Museu Histórico do Exército
Forte de Copacabana
Ponta de Copacabana
Praia do Diabo

0   500 m
0   500 yds

Copacabana, Ipanema and Leblon
Quick Reference Guide

Copacabana (▷ 18)

This is Rio's most popular and best-known beach neighbourhood; the wide arc of flat, white sand is flanked by high-rise hotels and apartment blocks and its streets are lined with lively bars, restaurants and cafés.

Ipanema (▷ 26)

The heartland of the city's coolest and trendiest set, Ipanema beach is the place to be seen. You can also witness a stunning sunset over the Dois Irmãos and Pedra da Gávea peaks, before heading out for the Ipanema nightlife.

Jardim Botânico (▷ 28)

Rio's Botanical Gardens were founded in the Imperial era and offer a peaceful retreat from the city bustle, with tall palms, giant Amazonian lily ponds and multi-coloured birdlife.

Lagoa (▷ 30)

This upscale inland neighbourhood fringes the Rodrigo de Freitas Lagoon, popular for its leisure boating as well as romantic lake-shore restaurants. There are also art galleries, a horse-racing track and some excellent parks.

MORE TO SEE   65

Forte de Copacabana
Fundação Eva Klabin

CITY TOURS

SHOP 114

Art and Handicrafts
O Sol
Books and Music
Bossanova & Companhia
Livraria Argumento
Toca de Vinicius
Fashion and Jewellery
Bumbum
Farm
Gilson Martins
Havaianas
Maria Oiticica
Museu H. Stern

Food, Drink and Markets
Feira de Antigüidades
Lidador
Miscellaneous
Brecho de Salto Alto
Parceria Carioca
Shopping Malls
Rio Design Leblon
Shopping Cassino Atlántico
Shopping Cidade de Copacabana
Shopping Leblon
Supermarkets
Zona Sul

ENTERTAINMENT 126

Arts/Cultural Centres
Oi Futuro Ipanema
Bars
Academia da Cachaça
Bar d'Hotel
Baretto Londra
Bip Bip
Devassa
Garota de Ipanema
Jobi

Clubs and Dancehalls
00
Baronneti
Boox
Bunker 94
Melt
Mistura Fina
Up
Concert Halls
Plataforma 1

EAT 138

Cafés and Bars
Bracarense
Café do Lage
Cervantes
Juice Co
Fusion
Le Pré Catelan
Roberta Sudbrack
Meat Feasts
Arab da Lagoa
Casa da Feijoada

Seafood
Fasano al Mare
Siri Mole & Cia
Vegetarian
Celeiro
Líquido
Mil Frutas
Vegetariano Social Clube

The Hills

The jungle-clad mountains towering over Rio are dominated by the city's most iconic symbol—the statue of Cristo Redentor on Corcovado. Nestled on the lower slopes is Santa Teresa, an upmarket arty neighbourhood with galleries, workshop studios and museums lining its winding cobbled streets.

Morning
Start your visit to **Santa Teresa** (▷ 58–59) at the downtown terminus of the tram station, near **Arcos da Lapa** (▷ 33). The little wooden trams— known in Rio as *bondes* (bon-jees)—are wonderfully rickety, old open-sided carriages, often overflowing with passengers hanging onto the sides. Take a tram to the **Largo dos Guimarães**, which is flanked by cafés and craft shops.

Mid-morning
Take a short detour down Rua Carlos Brant to the **tram depot**, which has a tiny tram museum. Walk or take another tram uphill to the **Museu da Chácara do Céu** (▷ 70), an elegant 1950s mansion and art gallery, with great views glimpsed from its garden. Close by is the **Centro Cultural Parque das Ruínas** (▷ 67), a cultural centre from whose balconies you get a stunning panorama over the hillsides.

Lunch
Santa Teresa has plenty of great eating options for lunch. You could try one of the many atmospheric old bars, such as **Bar do Mineiro** (▷ 143), **Bar do Gomez** (Rua Áurea 26) or **Bar do Arnaudo** (Rua Almirante Alexandrino 316), which serve good-value set meals *(pratos executivos)*.

CITY TOURS

Afternoon

Hop on a tram back to the city centre and take a bus (180 or 184) to the **Cosme Velho** train station. Funicular trains wind up from here through the lush Tijuca rainforest to the majestic **Cristo Redentor** statue (▷ 20–21).

Mid-afternoon

Explore the paths and lookout platforms on the summit of **Corcovado**; soak up the majestic views over the whole city and wait until sunset, when the statue is lit up in all its glory.

Early evening

Take a taxi down through the **Parque Nacional da Tijuca** (▷ 50), stopping en route at Mirante Dona Marta lookout point.

Dinner

Deep in the Tijuca forest is the charmingly rustic **Os Esquilos** restaurant (▷ 146), in a lovely old colonial villa in landscaped gardens. You can dine in peaceful splendour, with the hum of jungle wildlife as your background music.

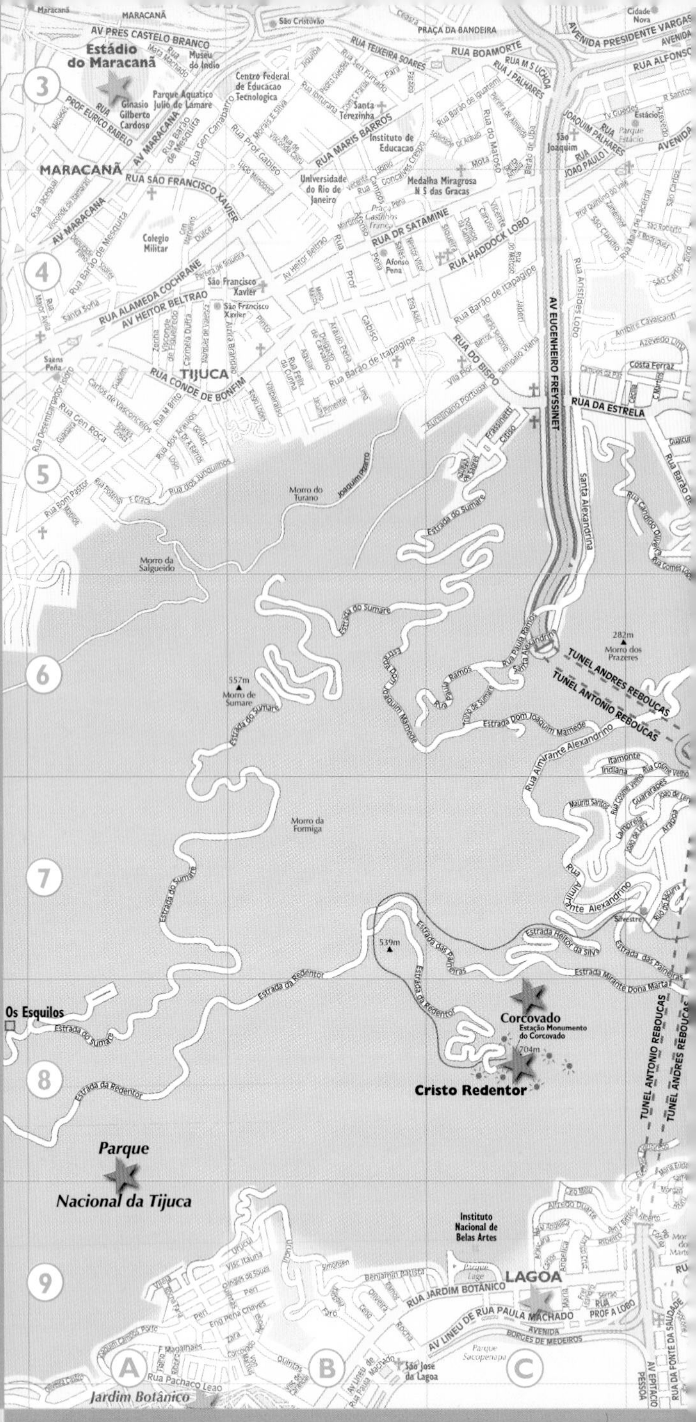
Estádio do Maracanã
MARACANÃ
AV PRES CASTELO BRANCO
Museu do Indio
Centro Federal de Educacao Tecnologica
Parque Aquatico Julio de Lamare
Ginasio Gilberto Cardoso
PRAÇA DA BANDEIRA
RUA TEIXEIRA SOARES
RUA BOAMORTE
AVENIDA PRESIDENTE VARGAS
RUA ALFONSO
Cidade Nova
Estácio
São Joaquim
RUA JOAO PAULO I
RUA MARIS BARROS
Santa Terezinha
Instituto de Educacao
Universidade do Rio de Janeiro
Medalha Miragrosa N S das Gracas
RUA SÃO FRANCISCO XAVIER
AV MARACANA
Colegio Militar
RUA DR SATAMINE
RUA HADDOCK LOBO
Afonso Pena
São Francisco Xavier
RUA ALAMEDA COCHRANE
AV HEITOR BELTRAO
Saens Peña
TIJUCA
RUA CONDE DE BONFIM
RUA DO BISPO
AV EUGENHEIRO FREYSSINET
RUA DA ESTRELA
Costa Ferraz
Morro do Turano
Estrada do Sumare
Morro da Salgueido
Santa Alexandrina
282m Morro dos Prazeres
TUNEL ANDRES REBOUCAS
TUNEL ANTONIO REBOUCAS
557m Morro de Sumare
Estrada Dom Joaquim Mamede
Rua Almirante Alexandrino
Morro da Formiga
539m
Estrada das Paineiras
Estrada da Redentor
Estrada Heitor da Silva
Estrada Mirante Dona Marta
Os Esquilos
Corcovado
Estação Monumento do Corcovado
704m
Cristo Redentor
Parque Nacional da Tijuca
Instituto Nacional de Belas Artes
LAGOA
RUA JARDIM BOTÂNICO
AV LINEU DE RUA PAULA MACHADO
AVENIDA BORGES DE MEDEIROS
Parque Sacopenapa
São José da Lagoa
Rua Pachaco Leao
Jardim Botânico
RUA DA FONTE DA SAUDADE
AV EPITACIO PESSOA
3
4
5
6
7
8
9
A
B
C

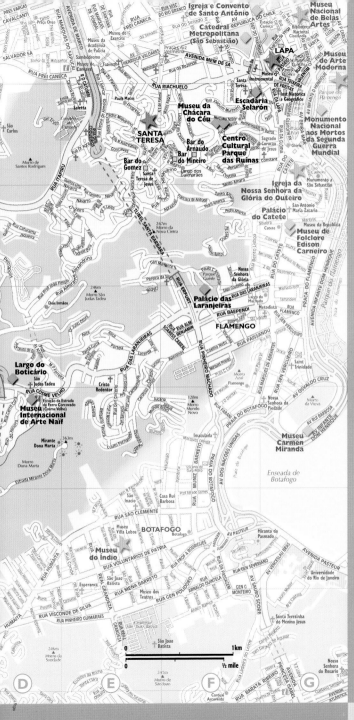

TOP 25 SIGHTS AND EXPERIENCES

Corcovado and Cristo Redentor (▷ 20)

The beautiful statue of Christ the Redeemer is Rio's most iconic symbol, looking over the city from its mountain-top perch. The ride on the funicular railway up Corcovado's lushly wooded slopes is an unmissable experience.

Lapa (▷ 32)

Lapa is the city's hub of bohemian culture, with dozens of top-quality live music venues, many of which are housed in converted old factories; if you like quirky shopping as well as full-on nightlife, here you can have both in the same place.

Parque Nacional da Tijuca (▷ 50)

This national park is the green blanket that wraps around the city, encompassing Corcovado and the highest peak, Pico da Tijuca. The superb site offers walkers hiking trails through pristine forest, past waterfalls and crystal-clear springs.

Santa Teresa (▷ 58)

This rambling, hilly residential district feels a world away from the busy beaches and downtown streets it overlooks. Santa Teresa is home to many musicians and artists, who base their studios in the large, elegantly faded colonial mansions.

CITY TOURS

CITY TOURS

Beach Suburbs

Rio's western suburbs are fringed with the city's longest, most uncrowded beaches; as well as its booming new residential areas, with ongoing construction work for the 2016 Olympic Village. As many of its attractions are spread far apart and off the beaten track, getting around by a combination of bus and taxi or hire car with driver is recommended.

Morning
Start your day with a guided walk around the magical **Sítio Roberto Burle Marx** (▷ 60–61; admission by pre-booked guided tour only, Tue–Sun 9.30, 1.30). The former home of Rio's foremost landscape designer is tucked away on a wooded hillside above Grumari. The grounds are acclaimed as one of the world's best tropical plant collections. The shady paths are still relatively cool in the morning air, but be sure to bring insect repellent.

Mid-morning
Take a taxi to the nearby **Parque Ecológico Chico Mendes** (▷ 72), one of Rio's last remaining areas of protected marshlands; if you're lucky you might spot one of its rare resident species, the *jacaré-de-papo-amarelo* (broad-nosed cayman). A little further inland (another short taxi ride) is one of Rio's most enchanting cultural exhibitions, the **Museu Casa do Pontal** (▷ 38–39); great fun for the whole family, particularly on a rainy day.

Lunch
Back to the coast, and the wide boulevards and shopping malls of **Barra da Tijuca** (▷ 66) offer a great range of eating choices. **Beco do Alemão** (▷ 143) is a no-frills roadside diner offering an excellent-value *por kilo* buffet, with grilled meats and fresh salads. You can enjoy Minas Gerais dishes there on Thursdays.

Afternoon
Relax on **Barra Beach**, or if you're feeling energetic, hire a bike and pedal along the seafront *ciclovia* (designated cycle track) to the **Lagoa de Marapendi** inland lagoon (bicycle rental agency: Cyclo Ponto, Barra da Tijuca, Avenida Olegário Maciel 45, tel 3153 3365; Mon–Sat 9–7; bicycle rental R$10 per hour/ R$40 per day). If you get too hot, have a free shower with the cunningly designed water sprays built into advertising boards that line the path.

Mid-afternoon
Mingle with the local young jet set, who like to chill out on **Praia do Pepê** (▷ 66); watch the hang-gliders land further along the beach and sip a smoothie at the **Barraca do Pepê** beach kiosk.

Early evening
Give your credit card a work-out and explore one of Barra's giant shopping malls; **Barra Shopping** (▷ 119) is the city's biggest, with outlets of local and international designer brands galore.

Dinner
The shopping malls also offer many surprisingly good-value restaurants, but for something special, **Nuth Lounge** (▷ 135) is one of Rio's most sophisticated nightclubs, with an equally smart restaurant. Or, for a more peaceful natural setting, **Point de Grumari** (▷ 149), in farthest Grumari, serves succulently fresh seafood with superb terrace views over the Sepetiba Lagoon.

①

ANCHIETA

Gericinó

Rio Sara puí

Rio do Pau

Rio Pavuna

AVENIDA BRASIL BR101

AVENIDA BRASIL

Rio Marangá

② Santissimo

Senador
Camara

SANTA

CRUZ

Bangu

Padre
Miguel

Magalhães
Bastos

Vila
Militar

Realengo

AV MARECHAL

AV
ALBERICO

AV

Senador
Vasconcelos

Rio Piraquara

Jardim
Sulacap

Rio

③

855m
▲
Morro de
Santa Bárbara

Rio Grande

Rio
do
Camorim

Rio Cabungui

Vargem
Grande

Camorim

AVENIDA SALVADOR ALLENDE

AVENIDA
ABELARDO

Rio Vargem Grande

Vargem
Pequena

Canal   do Portelo

Lagoa
de Jacarepaguá

④

Canal
do
Cortado

AVENIDA DAS AMÉRICAS

**Sítio Roberto
Burle Marx**

Canal de Sernambetiba

Recreio dos
Bandeirantes

AV DAS AMÉRICAS

**Museu Casa
do Pontal**

Lagoa   de   Marapendi AVENIDA SERNAMBETIBA

**Parque Ecológico
Chico Mendes**

Grumari

□ **Point de Grumari**

Oceano

⑤

ⓐ   ⓑ

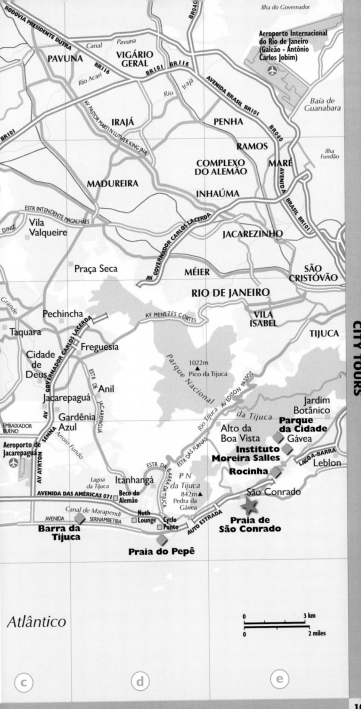

Ilha do Governador

Aeroporto Internacional do Rio de Janeiro (Galeão – Antônio Carlos Jobim)

RODOVIA PRESIDENTE DUTRA

Canal Pavuna

PAVUNA

BR116

VIGÁRIO GERAL

BR101 BR116

Rio Acari

AVENIDA BRASIL BR101

BR040

Baía de Guanabara

AV PASTOR MARTIN LUTHER KING JNR

IRAJÁ

Rio Irajá

PENHA

Ilha Fundão

BR101

RAMOS

MARÉ

COMPLEXO DO ALEMÃO

AVENIDA

MADUREIRA

INHAÚMA

BRASIL BR101

ESTR INTENDENTE MAGALHÃES

DINIZ

Vila Valqueire

JACAREZINHO

AV GOVERNADOR CARLOS LACERDA

Praça Seca

MÉIER

SÃO CRISTÓVÃO

RIO DE JANEIRO

Grande

Pechincha

AV MENEZES CORTES

VILA ISABEL

TIJUCA

Taquara

GOVERNADOR CARLOS LACERDA

Freguesia

Cidade de Deus

ESTR DE ANIL

Jacarepaguá

JACAREPAGUÁ

Gardênia Azul

AV AYRTON SENNA

EMBAIXADOR BUENO

Aeroporto de Jacarepaguá

Arroio Fundo

Parque Nacional

1022m ▲ Pico da Tijuca

da Tijuca

Rio Tijuca

AV EDSON PASSOS

Jardim Botânico

Parque da Cidade

Alto da Boa Vista

Gávea

Instituto Moreira Salles

LAGOA-BARRA

Leblon

Rocinha

Lagoa da Tijuca

Itanhangá

Beco do Alemão

ESTR DA BARRA DA TIJUCA

ESTR DAS FURNAS

P N da Tijuca

842m ▲ Pedra da Gávea

São Conrado

AVENIDA DAS AMÉRICAS 071

Nuth Lounge

Cyclo Ponto

AUTO ESTRADA

Praia de São Conrado

Canal de Marapendi

AVENIDA SERNAMBETIBA

Barra da Tijuca

Praia do Pepê

Atlântico

0 3 km

0 2 miles

c d e

105

TOP 25 SIGHTS AND EXPERIENCES

Museu Casa do Pontal (▷ 38)

This enchanting little museum is hidden in a quiet suburb, but is well worth a visit. It displays thousands of beautifully crafted figures collected from all over Brazil, which graphically illustrate the minutiae of traditional life. Children will enjoy pushing the buttons to make various scenes come alive, including a Carnaval parade. The museum is fascinating, a treat on a rainy day.

Praia de São Conrado (▷ 56)

Praia de São Conrado is one of the best surfing beaches in Rio and is among the most popular beaches in the western suburbs. (However, with strong currents, the water is not suitable for swimmers.) The booming modern neighbourhood of São Conrado also boasts some of the city's biggest shopping malls and the prestigious Gávea Golf and Country Club. Adventure activities include hang-gliding.

Sítio Roberto Burle Marx (▷ 60)

Stroll through gorgeous tropical gardens in the former home of Brazil's most important landscape designer, Roberto Burle Marx. See how many of the 3,500 tropical and semi-tropical plant species grown here you can spot. The house has been lovingly preserved as Burle Marx left it, and is full of his artwork and collections from the Americas.

MORE TO SEE 64

Barra da Tijuca
Instituto Moreira Salles
Parque da Cidade
Parque Ecológico Chico Mendes
Rocinha

SHOP 114

Books and Music
Fnac
Shopping Malls
Barra Shopping

Fashion Mall
New York City Center

ENTERTAINMENT 126

Clubs and Dancehalls
Castelo das Pedras
Nuth Lounge

Concert Halls
Cidade da Música
Citibank Hall
HSBC Arena

EAT 138

Cafés and Bars
Barraca do Pepê
European
Beco do Alemão
Meat Feasts
Tourão

Seafood
Point de Grumari
Skunna
Vegetarian
Delirio Tropical

Praia Recreio dos Bandeirantes, in Barra da Tijuca

Further Afield

Rio state offers anything from chic beach resorts and historic coffee plantations to the futuristic modern art museum at Niterói. If you choose to do the Búzios itinerary, below, it would be advisable to stay overnight. The Niterói tour can be done as a day trip.

DAY 1 Morning
Take a three-hour trip by air-conditioned coach or car to **Búzios** (▷ 14–15), a beautiful beach resort on a rocky peninsula some 180km (112 miles) northeast of Rio.

Mid-morning
Relax on **Praia da Armação**, one of the loveliest of the peninsula's twenty or so beaches, with boutiques and bars lining the cobblestone streets along the shore.

Lunch
Take your pick from dozens of beachside restaurants, cafés and snack-bars dotted around Rua das Pedras, the resort's busy hub, with heaps of fresh, tasty seafood on offer.

Afternoon
Explore Búzios on the guided **Búzios Trolley**, with stops en route at look-out points offering awesome views of its gorgeous sandy beaches and secluded bays.

Early evening
Spot the celebs at trendy **Chez Michou** (▷ 133), and toast the sunset with a caipirinha cocktail.

Dinner
Manguinhos, a fishing village on the neck of the peninsula, has a cluster of romantic open-air restaurants under the trees around the fish market. The pick of the bunch has to be the **Bar dos Pescadores** (▷ 143), which is decorated with portraits of revered local fishermen.

DAY 2 Morning

Take a taxi or catch a bus (741 from Copacabana and Praça XV, downtown) around Guanabara Bay to **Niterói** (▷ 44–45), a city of some half a million inhabitants, linked to Rio via the road bridge.

Mid-morning

Visit the **Museu de Arte Contemporânea** (▷ 44–45), housed in one of the most spectacular works by modern architect Oscar Niemeyer.

Lunch

Tucked away in Portugal Pequeno, Niterói's old dockside area, is the **Mercado de Peixe São Pedro** (▷ 150, panel), the fish market supplying all of Rio. Buy your fish here, then take it upstairs, where simple but good-quality restaurants will cook and serve it for you.

Afternoon

Explore the **Fortaleza de Santa Cruz da Barra**, one of the many old fortresses defending Baia de Guanabara. From its rocky perch you almost feel you could reach across the bay and touch Sugarloaf.

Mid-afternoon

Take a taxi up to the **Parque da Cidade** (▷ 72), a forested park spread high over the city. Sunset from up here is spectacular.

Dinner

Icaraí is Niterói's smart beachside neighbourhood, with many restaurants lining the seafront. One of the most popular places to eat is **Porcão Niterói** (▷ 149), a branch of Porcão Rio's—an all-you-can-eat *churrascaria*—at half the price of the famous original (▷ 149).

Evening

Return to Rio by road, or hop on a ferry from the Charitas terminal (another Niemeyer design), from where there are regular departures across the bay to the downtown ferry port near Praça XV.

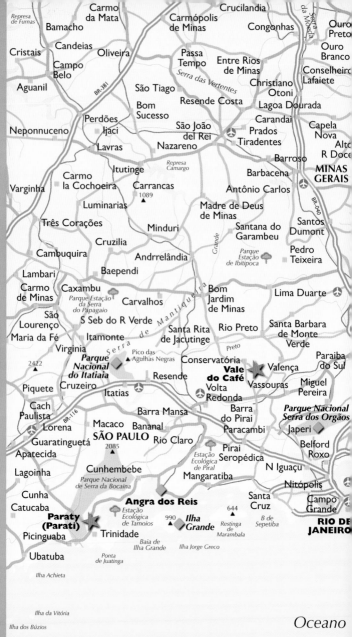

Mariana
Rio Doce
Jequeri
Manhuaçu
Martins Soares
Lajinha
BR-262
Ponte Nova
Sta Margarida
Ibatiba
Manhumirim
Sericita
2890
Pico da Bandeira
Lúna
Piranga
Canaã
Araponga
Divino
Parque Nacional da Caparaó
Muniz Freire
Viçosa
Espera Feliz
Ibitirama
Sen Firmino
Coimbra
Ervália
Glória
Anutiba
Rio Espera
Carangola
ESPÍRITO SANTO
Divinesia
Visconde do R Branco
Miradouro
Guaçuí
Alegre
Ubá
Porciúncula
Varre-Saí
Muqui
Marces
Muriaé
Eugenópolis
Natividade
Mimoso do Sul
Rio Pomba
Mirai
Patrocinio Itaperuna
do Muriaé
726
Bom Jesus
Tabulero
Guarani
Cataguases
Pedra do Baú
Ponte de Itabapoana
Novo
S João Nepomuceno
Palma
Miracema
Cnl Pacheco
Leopoldina
S Antônio de Padua
Italva
Cons Josino
Juiz de Fora
Cardoso Moreira
Matias Barbosa
Bicas
Volte Grande
Aperibe
Itaocara
Travessão
Mar de Espanha
Euclidelandia
Grande
São Fidelis
Paraiba do Sul
Alem Paraiba
1576
P São Mateus
Campos
Sapucaia
Cantagalo
Santa Maria Madalena
Lago Cima
Ibitiana
Três Rios
RIO DE JANEIRO
Cordeiro
Tocos
Duas Barras
Conceição de Macabu
Posse
Cons Paulino
1429
Carapebus
Lago Feia
Quiçamã
Serra dos Orgãos
Nova Friburgo
Cabionas
Cascatinha
Lumiar
Parque Nacional da Restinga de Jurubatiba
Petrópolis
Teresópolis
Casimiro de Abreu
Barra de Macaé
R B do Tingua
Cachoeiras de Macacu
806
Macaé
Majé
Japuiba
Rio das Ostras
Ilha de Santana
R B do Poço das Antas
Neves
Rio Bonito
Barra de São João
Itabora
São Vicente de Paula
Ipijba
São Pedro
Cabo dos Búzios
Niterói
Araruama
Armação dos Búzios (Búzios)
Ponta Negra
Saquarema
Cabo Frio
Lago de Araruama
Arraial do Cabo
Ilha do Cabo Frio

Atlântico

0   50 km
0   30 miles

CITY TOURS

111

SIGHTS AND EXPERIENCES

Búzios (▷ 14)
On a rocky peninsula fringed with sandy beaches, Búzios is a former fishing village 'discovered' by Brigitte Bardot in the 1960s and now a chic resort.

Cabo Frio (▷ 16)
A large-scale resort east of Rio, Cabo Frio has wide beaches backed by sand dunes. Its nearby headland, Arraial do Cabo, is world-famous for top diving sites.

Niterói (▷ 44)
Rio's unsung neighbour across the bay enjoys superior views of the city's highlights. Attractions include the breathtaking Museu de Arte Contemporânea.

Paraty (▷ 48)
This UNESCO-protected colonial port is a picturesque gem on the Costa Verde between Rio and São Paulo, with art galleries, boutiques, and bars serving fine cachaça.

Petrópolis (▷ 52)
The Imperial Palace in this city offers an insight into an era when Rio was the capital of the Portuguese Empire, complete with all its aristocratic trappings.

Vale do Café (▷ 62)
This region of rolling green hills and valleys, a couple of hours' drive from Rio, shelters former coffee *fazendas* (plantations) that now welcome visitors.

MORE TO SEE 64

Angra dos Reis
Ilha Grande
Parque Nacional Itatiaia
Parque Nacional Serra dos Orgãos

SHOP 114

Art and Handicrafts
Arte Marinha
Atelier da Terra
Cerâmica Luiz Salvador
Ivonne R
Books and Music
Armasom de Búzios

Fashion and Jewellery
Catalina
Food, Drink and Markets
Empório da Cachaça
Mundo Verde
Miscellaneous
Loja do Brasil

ENTERTAINMENT 126

Arts/Cultural Centres
Casa da Cultura
Bars
Bar Tom Maior
Taberna Dom Beto
Cinemas and Theatres
Gran Cine Bardot
Teatro Espaço

Clubs and Dancehalls
Chez Michou
Privilege

EAT 138

Brazilian
Arcadia Bistrô Imperatriz
Bordeaux Vinhos & Cia
A Mineira
Pousada da Alcobaca
Cafés and Bars
Chocolate Katz
European
Brigitta's
Oliveiras da Serra
Punto di Vino

Fusion
Sawasdee
Meat Feasts
Porcão Niterói
Por Kilo Restaurants
Boom
Familia Paludo
Seafood
Banana da Terra
Bar dos Pescadores

CITY TOURS

Shop

Whether you're looking for the best local products, a shopping mall or a quirky boutique, you'll find them all in Rio de Janeiro. In this section, shops are listed alphabetically.

SHOP

Introduction

Cosmopolitan Rio has a wealth of shopping opportunities, from vibrant street markets to garish souvenir shops, from chic boutiques to vast, sophisticated malls. Best buys include designer fashion, daring beachwear, handicrafts, jewellery, beauty products, precious gemstones and music, as well as food delicacies.

Malls and Markets

Shopping malls, air-conditioned, spacious and safe, offer a comfortable if somewhat sanitized shopping experience, and often with prices and quality to compete with main-street stores. From Botafogo through Zona Sul to Barra, each of the beach neighbourhoods has at least one mall, many of which offer free transport to and from major hotels. There are also several open-air street markets dotted around the city. Some markets specialize, including the popular Feira Hippy Market in Ipanema, which sells touristy handicrafts, jewellery and clothes; and Lapa's monthly antiques market (▷ opposite).

What to Buy Where

Downtown is the best area to find cut-price clothes and a huge range of other goods—as long as you don't mind the crowds. The enormous Saara market (▷ 121, panel) is a sprawling labyrinth of stalls spread around Rua da Alfândega. You can buy everything here:

TIPS

● Prices are comparable to Europe and the US, but particularly good-value buys include Havaianas and local crafts. Haggling, politely, is expected in markets and street stalls.

● Avoid using large denomination notes, particularly in markets and street stalls. And count your change carefully.

● The international airport's duty-free shops are open both to arriving and departing passengers; prices are much higher than in most shops in the city, however.

Clockwise from top: Wandering through Ipanema's Hippy Market; souvenirs of Rio abound; a market trader sells corn-on-the-cob; O Sol handicraft shop in Jardim

SHOP

from clothes and sunglasses to CDs and cheap MP3 players. It's packed and chaotic, so leave valuables behind. Bohemian Lapa is the best area in the city for browsing around converted warehouses and factories for antiques and bric-a-brac; the Feira do Rio Antigo is an antiques market in Rua do Lavradio on the first Saturday of the month (▷ 123, panel). Or if you'd like to combine shopping with nightlife, the amazing Rio Scenarium (▷ 136) hosts some of Rio's best live music shows, with antiques lining its bare brick walls. Santa Teresa is a good area for browsing art studios and good-quality handicraft and antique shops. Its tranquil, cobbled backstreets make for a more pleasant shopping experience than the traffic-clogged Centro and Zona Sul. Likewise, Ipanema and Leblon also have some excellent specialist stores on their quieter side roads, particularly those focusing on music, art and designer fashion.

Food and Drink

Supermarkets are definitely your best bet for food and drink, with the larger outlets stocking a wide range of goods at much cheaper prices than in souvenir shops. (Bear in mind, though, that you cannot take fresh fruit and vegetables out of the country.) Recommended items include coffee, either ground or beans, herbal teas and other tropical products. Cachaça—cane rum—is also a good buy. Reputable brands include Velho Barreiro, 51 and São Francisco. Or choose from a colourful array of liqueurs.

ON THE BEACH

Beachwear is a very attractive buy, with skimpy costumes available from beach vendors and boutiques. Must-haves range from the almost invisible *fio dental* (dental floss!) bikinis to more modestly cut *sunkinis*, a cross between a bikini and the *sunga*—Speedo-style shorts. Apart from surfers, few men wear Bermudas.

Botânico; the luxury Shopping Leblon mall; designer bags at Gilson Martins

Directory

Downtown and Northern Rio

Art and Handicrafts
O Equilibrista
Pé de Boi
Food, Drink and Markets
Saara (▷ 121, panel)
Shopping Malls
Vertical Shopping

Copacabana, Ipanema and Leblon

Art and Handicrafts
O Sol
Books and Music
Bossanova & Companhia
Livraria Argumento
Toca de Vinicius
Fashion and Jewellery
Bumbum
Farm
Gilson Martins
Havaianas
Maria Oiticica
Museu H. Stern
Food, Drink and Markets
Feira de Antigüidades
Lidador
Miscellaneous
Brecho de Salto Alto
Parceria Carioca
Shopping Malls
Rio Design Leblon
Shopping Cassino Atlántico
Shopping Cidade de Copacabana
Shopping Leblon
Supermarket
Zona Sul

The Hills

Art and Handicrafts
Cena Urbana
Do Século Passado
Mariana Zareth
Pé de Boi
Trilhos Urbanos
La Vereda
Books and Music
Largo das Letras
Plano B
Food, Drink and Markets
Dom Faustino
Feira do Rio Antigo (▷ 123, panel)
Magnífica Cachaça do Brasil

Beach Suburbs

Books and Music
Fnac
Shopping Malls
Barra Shopping
Fashion Mall
New York City Center

Further Afield

Art and Handicrafts
Arte Marinha
Atelier da Terra
Cerâmica Luiz Salvador
Ivonne R
Books and Music
Armasom de Búzios
Fashion and Jewellery
Catalina
Food, Drink and Markets
Empório da Cachaça
Mundo Verde
Miscellaneous
Loja do Brasil

SHOP

Shopping A–Z

ARMASOM DE BÚZIOS
This excellent little music shop sells a wide range of jazz, blues and MPB *(Música Popular Brasileira)* CDs, including recordings of local concerts.

🔲 Map, ▷ 111 ✉ Rua das Pedras 25, Búzios ☎ (22) 2623 6799

ARTE MARINHA
Arte Marinha is a handicrafts shop specializing in carved wooden fish, ornaments and all things inspired by the sea. The items are bought direct from local artisans in Cabo Frio's Jardim Esperança community.

🔲 Map, ▷ 111 ✉ Avenida José Bento Ribeiro Dantas 1144, Praia da Armação, Búzios ☎ (22) 2623 2332

ATELIER DA TERRA
Beautiful hand-painted model boats, leaf-shaped oars and other wooden handicrafts are sold here, made by the indigenous community from Saco do Mamanguã, the tropical fjord beyond Paraty Bay.

🔲 Map, ▷ 110 ✉ Rua da Lapa 1, Paraty ☎ (24) 3371 3070

BARRA SHOPPING
www.barrashopping.com.br
Rio's biggest mall has hundreds of boutiques and department stores, as well as restaurants, a bowling

IPANEMA
The heart of Ipanema's shopping district is around Rua Visconde de Pirajá, with side street Rua Garcia d'Avila clustered with luxury jewellery shops and chic boutiques; there are also many trendy bars and street cafés in the area, where you can take a break before giving your credit card another workout.

alley, cinema, playground and the Hot Zone amusement area, with white-knuckle rides.

🔲 Map, ▷ 105 c4 ✉ Avenida das Américas 4666, Barra da Tijuca ☎ 3089 1000 🕐 Mon–Sat 10–10, Sun 1–9 🚌 175, 177

BOSSANOVA & COMPANHIA
www.bossanovaecompanhia.com.br
This fascinating little music shop sells books, CDs, sheet music and musical instruments. Clubs—now closed—on this alley spawned the cult for samba in the 1960s; black-and-white photos and album covers line the walls, in tribute to past stars.

🔲 F10 ✉ Rua Duvivier 37A, Copacabana ☎ 2295 8096 🚇 Cardeal Arcoverde

BRECHO DE SALTO ALTO
Think loud-print shirts and dresses at this store, which sells retro fashion for men and women from the 1950s, '60s and '70s, plus kitsch art deco ornaments, pop art lampshades and vintage vinyl LPs.

🔲 F10 ✉ Rua Siqueira Campos 143, Loja 44, Copacabana ☎ 2236 2589 🚇 Siqueira Campos

BUMBUM
www.bumbum.com.br
As its name not-so-subtly suggests, this chic designer-label boutique has some of Rio's most revealing beachwear for men and women.

🔲 D12 ✉ Rua Visconde de Pirajá 351, Loja B ☎ 2287 9951 🚇 Ipanema/General Osório

CATALINA
www.aguia.com.br
Buy stylish designer bikinis and one-piece costumes, made by a long-established fashion company

Some of the best shopping malls are in Copacabana, Ipanema and Leblon; mainstream designer names dominate but you can also find small specialists, such as the antiques and jewellery shops in the Cassino Atlântico. Malls are a good way to spend a rainy day; most are open until late at weekends and some, such as Shopping Leblon, offer free transport to and from Zona Sul hotels.

based in Petrópolis. There are also Havaianas, sandals and jewellery.
➕ Map, ▷ 111 ✉ Rua das Pedras 73, Loja A, Búzios ☎ (22) 2623 6158

CENA URBANA

http://integracaocenaurbana.anepsrj.com
A not-for-profit cultural foundation based in Santa Teresa, Cena Urbana supports artists from deprived backgrounds. The paintings on display focus on Carnaval, the environment and popular culture.
➕ E4 ✉ Travessa do Oriente 111, Santa Teresa ☎ 2221 4608 ⏰ Tue–Sun 11–6
🚋 Tram to Largo dos Guimarães

CERÂMICA LUIZ SALVADOR

www.ceramicaluizsalvador.com.br
This ceramics factory specializes in *azulejos,* the faience-style blue-and-white tiles seen in colonial churches across Brazil. It also runs fascinating tours, showing the artisans' traditional skills, and the firing and glazing processes.
➕ Map, ▷ 111 ✉ Estrada União e Indústria 10588, Itaipava, Petrópolis ☎ (24) 2232 2500 ⏰ Sun–Thu 10–6, Fri–Sat 10–8

DO SÉCULO PASSADO

This huge antiques store in the heart of Lapa's monthly market street is ideal for browsers in search of that surprise treasure. Dusty back rooms are full of giant gilt picture frames, religious icons, kitsch ornaments and much more.
➕ F3 ✉ Rua do Lavradio 106, Lapa ☎ 2252 2770 🚇 Cinelândia

DOM FAUSTINO

There's a beautiful array of herbs, spices and bottled preserves at this immaculate deli and café.

Designer bags at Gilson Martins

There's no shortage of fashion boutiques in Rio

Buffet-style snacks are served at tables in the back.

🔲 F3 ✉ Rua Riachuelo 126, Lapa ☎ 2224 9896 🚌 433, 464

EMPÓRIO DA CACHAÇA

The shelves in this tiny but wonderful deli and liquor store are packed high with many brands of cachaça (cane rum), as well as preserved fruit and vegetables in ornamental jars.

🔲 Map, ▷ 110 ✉ Rua Dr Samuel Costa 22, Paraty ☎ (24) 3371 6329

O EQUILIBRISTA

Browse a selection of ethnic artefacts, naïve art, jewellery, ornaments, books and toys.

🔲 G3 ✉ Centro Cultural da Justiça Federal, Avenida Rio Branco 241, Centro ☎ 2532 3605 🕐 Tue–Sun 12–7 🚇 Cinelândia

FARM

www.farmrio.com.br

The colourful, casual, women's fashion and accessories sold here are popular and reasonably priced; there are other branches in Rio.

🔲 D12 ✉ Rua Visconde de Pirajá 365, Lojas C and D, Ipanema ☎ 2522 0023 🚇 Ipanema/General Osório

FASHION MALL

www.scfashionmall.com.br

A sophisticated, upmarket mall of modest proportions, Fashion Mall is popular for its high-quality deli-cafés, restaurants and cinema.

🔲 Map, ▷ 105 e4 ✉ Estrada da Gávea 899, São Conrado ☎ 2111 4444 🕐 Mon–Sat 10–10, Sun 3–9 🚌 177, 178

FEIRA DE ANTIGÜIDADES

One of the best antiques markets in Rio has 80 stalls selling a wide mix of objets d'art, porcelain, glass and crystal, silverware, paintings, collectible books and magazines.

🔲 A10–11 ✉ Praça Santos Dumont, opposite the Jockey Club 🕐 Sun 9–5 🚌 571, 573, 583

FNAC

www.fnac.com.br

This excellent bookshop in the Barra Shopping mall also sells music CDs and DVDs, with an internet café, as well as live music and book-signing events.

🔲 Map, ▷ 105 c4 ✉ Avenida das Américas 4666, Barra da Tijuca ☎ 2109 2000 🕐 Mon–Sat 10–10, Sun 1–9 🚌 175, 177

GILSON MARTINS

www.gilsonmartins.com.br

Artist Gilson Martin's imaginative handbags, wallets and accessories in bright colours and fun shapes are made from recycled materials.

🔲 D12 ✉ Rua Visconde de Pirajá 462 and 565, Ipanema ☎ 2275 8950 🚇 Ipanema/General Osório

HAVAIANAS

http://br.havaianas.com

This store sells the original and most fashionable flip-flops, with

SHOP

colour-coded racks of hundreds of designs, from basic to rhinestone-studded kitsch.

🔢 E11 ✉ Rua Xavier da Silveira 19, Loja B, Copacabana ☎ 2267 2418 🚇 Cantagalo

IVONNE R

In her workshop opposite the beach, Ivonne R makes wonder-fully wacky papier-mâché sculptures, as well as a variety of Carnaval masks, platform shoes, frogs and larger-than-life-size human figures, painted in lurid pop art colours.

🔢 Map, ▷ 111 ✉ Travessa Sant'Anna 32, Praia de Armação, Búzios ☎ (22) 2623 1495

LARGO DAS LETRAS

www.largodasletras.com.br
In an old mansion overlooking Largo dos Guimarães, this well-stocked little bookshop sells anything from fiction to art, history and travel books, along with some English paperbacks. There's also a cosy coffee bar at the back.

🔢 F4 ✉ Rua Almirante Alexandrino 501, Santa Teresa ☎ 2221 8992 🕐 Tue–Sat 2–10, Sun 2–8 🚋 Tram to Largo dos Guimarães

LIDADOR

www.lidador.com.br
This long-established liquor store and deli chain is a good place to

RUM

Paraty is one of the best places in Brazil for buying cachaça, which has been made here since the 17th century. Some distilleries (engenhos) are open to visitors, including the Engenho d'Ouro, 8km (5 miles) from Paraty, on the old Estrada Real, with free tastings (☎ (24) 9905 8268).

buy cachaça (cane rum), and many other spirits and wines, both local and international labels.

🔢 E10 ✉ Rua Barata Ribeiro 505, Copacabana ☎ 2549 0091 🚇 Siqueira Campos

LIVRARIA ARGUMENTO

www.livrariaargumento.com.br
Browse through a broad range of titles at this literary bookshop, which also has a café, music CDs and authors' events.

🔢 A12 ✉ Rua Dias Ferreira 417, Leblon ☎ 2239 5294 🕐 Daily until midnight 🚌 157, 292, 432, 435

LOJA DO BRASIL

From tiny tags on Havaianas to the yellow-and-green strip worn by the national football team, the Brazilian flag is a globally recognized symbol. This smart little shop offers every imaginable piece of merchandise adorned with the national colours, from beach towels to backpacks, beer coolers and key rings.

🔢 Map, ▷ 111 ✉ Rua Manoel Turibio de Farias 182, Búzios ☎ (22) 2623 3696

MAGNÍFICA CACHAÇA DO BRASIL

www.cachacamagnifica.com.br
This specialist liquor store sells its own high-quality brand of cachaça (cane rum) produced at the Fazenda do Anil in the Vale do Café (▷ 62–63).

🔢 E4 ✉ Rua Felício dos Santos 32, Santa Teresa ☎ 2508 9042 🚌 214. Tram to Largo dos Guimarães

MARIA OITICICA

www.mariaoiticica.com.br
Come here for high-quality, environmentally friendly jewellery,

with bracelets and necklaces made of silver, sustainable wood and fibres. The store supports community artisans throughout Brazil.

🕂 B12 ✉ Avenida Afranio de Mello Franco 290, Loja 112b, Leblon ☎ 3875 8025
🚌 404, 460A, 474, 476, 503A

MARIANA ZARETH

www.marianazareth.com.br
An unusual mix of local landscape paintings and abstract works with an Andean theme are the speciality at this art gallery with an open studio.

🕂 F4 ✉ Rua Almirante Alexandrino 342, Santa Teresa ☎ 2221 2257 🚃 Tram to Largo dos Guimarães

MUNDO VERDE

www.mundoverde.com.br
Organic foods, including coffee, bread, deli cheeses and bottled preserves, are sold here. It's a good place to buy delicacies from the nearby Vale dos Gourmets. There are other branches around Rio.

🕂 Map, ▷ 111 ✉ Rua do Imperador 864, Petrópolis ☎ (24) 2242 7788

▷ 111

SANTA TERESA AND LAPA

Santa Teresa has a growing number of art galleries and handicraft shops dotted around the winding streets. The best shopping to be had in Lapa is around Rua do Lavradio, where there are many antiques and bric-a-brac shops. The area comes alive the first Saturday of the month for the Feira do Rio Antigo, an all-day market with more than 300 stalls; plus live entertainment into the late hours.

MUSEU H. STERN

www.hstern.com.br
Brazil's best-known jeweller has branches worldwide. This glitzy Ipanema store offers workshop tours and has a gallery of precious stones, with free transport to and from major hotels.

🕂 D12 ✉ Rua Visconde de Pirajá 490, Ipanema ☎ 2274 3447 🚇 Ipanema/General Osório

NEW YORK CITY CENTER

www.nycc.com.br
This US-style entertainment centre provoked some local opposition with its miniature version of the

Edible treats at Ipanema's fruit and veg market

Colourful cushions for sale at the Friday market in Praca XV de Novembro

Statue of Liberty. One of the best of Barra's 30 or so malls, it has shops, 18 cinema screens, live entertainment and restaurants.
🗺 Map, ▷ 105 c4 ✉ Avenida das Américas 5000, Barra da Tijuca ☎ 2432 4980 🕐 Mon–Sat 10–10, Sun 3–9 (restaurants until 10) 🚌 175, 179, 523

PARCERIA CARIOCA

A not-for-profit organization, Parceria Carioca sells products made by teenagers living in deprived communities on the outskirts of Rio. Items include fun T-shirts, necklaces and handbags.
🗺 B9 ✉ Rua Jardim Botânico 728, Loja 108, Jardim Botânico ☎ 2259 1437 🚌 179, 571, 573, 583

PÉ DE BOI

www.pedeboi.com.br
High-quality handmade items from all over Brazil are sold here, particularly from Pernambuco and Minas Gerais: wooden carvings, ceramics, sculpture, textiles and antique collectibles (there's another branch on Rua Ipiranga 55, Laranjeiras).
🗺 G2 ✉ Rua da Assembléia 10, Centro ☎ 2232 7038 🕐 Mon–Fri 9–7 🚇 Carioca
🗺 F6 ✉ Rua da Ipiranga 55, Laranjeiras ☎ 2285 4395 🕐 Mon–Fri 9–7, Sat 9–1 🚇 Largo do Machado

PLANO B

A funky music shop between Lapa and Santa Teresa, Plano B sells an eclectic mix of new CDs and second-hand jazz LPs.
🗺 F3 ✉ Rua Francisco Muratori 2, Santa Teresa ☎ 2507 9860 🚌 214, 572

RIO DESIGN LEBLON

www.riodesign.com.br.
This upmarket shopping mall has mostly designer-label fashion and jewellery stores, including Camila Klein, Natan and Manufact. You can choose from nine restaurants.
🗺 B12 ✉ Avenida Ataulfo de Paiva 270, Leblon ☎ 3206 9100 🕐 Mon–Sat 10–10, Sun 3–9 🚌 571, 583, 584

SHOPPING CASSINO ATLÂNTICO

www.shoppingcassinoatlantico.com.br
A small mall handily located next to the Sofitel hotel, this place is mostly dedicated to upmarket art, jewellery and antiques (there's a market on Saturday 10–7).
🗺 E12 ✉ Avenida Atlântica 4240, Copacabana ☎ 2523 8709 🚇 Cantagalo

SHOPPING CIDADE DE COPACABANA

www.shoppingcidadecopacabana.com.br
One of Rio's first malls has a wide mix of shops, from antiques to design, plus quirky specialists.
🗺 F10 ✉ Rua Siqueira Campos 143, Copacabana ☎ 2255 3461 🕐 Mall daily 24 hours (but not all shops) 🚇 Siqueira Campos

SHOPPING LEBLON

www.shoppingleblon.com.br
This luxury mall with brand-name boutiques also has a bookshop, cinema and restaurants with views over Lagoa Rodrigo de Freitas.
🗺 B12 ✉ Avenida Afranio de Melo Franco 290, Leblon ☎ 3138 8000 🕐 Restaurants open until 1am Fri–Sat, until midnight Sun–Thu 🚌 404, 460A, 474, 476, 503A

O SOL

www.artesanato-sol.com.br
A not-for-profit handicraft store, O Sol supports apprentices from all over Brazil. Items for sale include furniture, folk-art chess

sets and ceramics from Marajoara, in the northern state of Pará.

🟦 B9 ✉ Rua Corcovado 213, Jardim Botânico ☎ 2294 5099 🚌 125, 409

TOCA DE VINICIUS
www.tocadovinicius.com.br
The owner of this music shop is a renowned musicologist. Choose from books, instruments, sheet music, CDs and DVDs.

🟦 D12 ✉ Rua Vinicius de Moraes 129, Ipanema ☎ 2247 5227 🚇 Ipanema/General Osório

TRILHOS URBANOS
This great little gallery and handi-crafts shop sells a range of local artworks, along with decorative picture frames, music CDs and carved wooden and ceramic ornaments.

🟦 F4 ✉ Rua Almirante Alexandrino 402, Santa Teresa ☎ 2242 3632 🚋 Tram to Largo dos Guimarães

LA VEREDA
www.lavereda.com.br
A few steps from the Largo dos Guimarães, this small craft shop

has good-quality modern art, handicrafts, books, photographs, stationery and music CDs.

🟦 F4 ✉ Rua Almirante Alexandrino 428, Santa Teresa ☎ 2507 0317 🚋 Tram to Largo dos Guimarães

VERTICAL SHOPPING
www.shoppingvertical.com.br
This is the only decent shopping mall in downtown. As well as shops, there are half a dozen cafés and restaurants, in a smartly converted 1950s office block.

🟦 F2 ✉ Rua Sete de Setembro 48, Centro ☎ 2224 0697 🕐 Mon–Fri 9–8 🚇 Carioca

ZONA SUL
www.zonasul.com.br
This chain of much loved super-markets, some of which also offer hot pizzas and breakfasts, is found throughout the city. Visit for fresh fruit and water for the beach, or for food stocks if you are in self-catering accommodation.

🟦 E12 ✉ Zona Rua Francisco Sá 35 ☎ 2247 9212 🕐 Mon–Thu 6.30am–10pm, Fri–Sat 6.30am–midnight, Sun 7am–10pm 🚇 General Osório

Bossanova & Companhia music shop, in Copacabana

The Shopping Leblon mall

Entertainment

Once you've done with sightseeing for the day, you'll find lots of other great things to do with your time in this chapter, even if all you want to do is relax with a drink. In this section, establishments are listed alphabetically.

Introduction

Rio offers a wealth of entertainment, from local dance halls to glitzy Carnaval shows. *Cariocas* start partying late at night, with few places coming alive before 10pm, and some going on until dawn. By day, you can often catch informal performances of music and dance on the beach, or, to escape the heat, there are surprisingly good-quality live concerts in the many air-conditioned shopping malls.

Entertainment Zones

Traditionally, the entertainment scene in Rio has been concentrated in Copacabana, Ipanema and Leblon, with everything from a cosy jazz club to a giant showhall featuring shimmying dancers wearing little else but plumes and sequins. Leme, at the eastern end of Copacabana, was once notorious for its seedy red-light district, but is enjoying a recent revival.

New Kids on the Block

In more recent years, lesser-known areas have spawned their own cultural scene, adding a bit of diversity to the mainstream favourites. In particular, Lapa (▷ 32–33) has become the place to hear live music. Atmospheric clubs in old warehouses play some of the city's best sounds. Wander Lapa's streets and you can pick between samba, *chorinho*, *forró* and even

CARNAVAL SHOWS

Carnaval samba schools put on live shows throughout most of the year, plus free rehearsals in the weeks leading up to Carnaval. Many of these are off the beaten track, so you're best advised to go with specialist tour agencies. The purpose-built Cidade do Samba (▷ 67) hosts excellent live shows on Thursday nights. Plataforma I (▷ 135) stages spectacular Carnaval shows nightly, including a medley of other popular Brazilian dance styles.

Clockwise from top: A Carnaval ball in Lapa; a classic caipirinha; looking down on Rio's night scene from Sugarloaf mountain; wandering through Lapa, a good

reggae and rock. One of Lapa's cultural focal points is the Arcos da Lapa, where the Fundição Progresso (▷ 134) and Circo Voador (▷ 133) arts centres put on cutting-edge shows and workshops. Santa Teresa also hosts occasional parties and live music in its cosy cafés and bars, offering a more laidback vibe. And the *favelas* have their very own DJ-driven scene: *Baile funk carioca* parties blast out heavy bass sounds, attracting a younger, more adventurous following (though never go to a *favela* without an official guide, ▷ 73, 132).

Market Music

Rio's markets, such as the Feira do Rio Antigo (▷ 123, panel) and the Feira de São Cristóvão (▷ 67), host some wonderful live music. You can see big-stage performances of northeastern Brazil's rich musical repertoire, and displays of *capoeira*, the mesmerizing Afro-Brazilian dance.

Listings

Entertainment listings appear in Friday newspaper supplements: *O Globo* has *Rio Show*; *Jornal do Brasil* has *Programa*; Sunday's *Veja* magazine has *Veja Rio*. The free *Rio Guide* is widely available in hotels and tourist offices. Also check websites such as www.riothisweek.com, www.riofesta.com.br, www.samba-choro.com.br and www.lanalapa.com.br.

LEARN TO SAMBA

To visit Rio and not dance the samba would be on a par with not going to Corcovado or Sugarloaf. Luckily, the city is full of *gafieiras*—traditional dance halls where locals will happily help you learn the intricate moves of *samba de salão*—ballroom samba. *Gafieiras* are friendly, casual ballrooms, and are dotted all over the city, with many concentrated in Lapa; one of the oldest is Estudantina, on Praca Tiradentes, in the city centre.

place to go for live music; bossa nova in Ipanema

Directory

Downtown and Northern Rio

Cinemas and Theatres
Theatro Municipal
Clubs and Dancehalls
Circo Voador
Elite
Estudantina
The Week
Concert Halls
Fundição Progresso

Baia de Guanabara

Concert Halls
Canecão
Music Festivals
Verão do Morro

Copacabana, Ipanema and Leblon

Arts/Cultural Centres
Oi Futuro Ipanema
Bars
Academia da Cachaça
Bar d'Hotel
Baretto Londra
Bip Bip
Devassa
Garota de Ipanema
Jobi
Clubs and Dancehalls
00
Baronneti
Boox
Bunker 94
Melt
Mistura Fina
Up
Concert Halls
Plataforma 1

The Hills

Arts/Cultural Centres
Centro Cultural Casa Rosa
Bars
Bar da Ladeira
Carioca da Gema
O Semente
Cinemas and Theatres
Cine Santa Teresa
Clubs and Dancehalls
Clube dos Democráticos
Rio Scenarium
Concert Halls
Sala Cecília Meireles

Beach Suburbs

Clubs and Dancehalls
Castelo das Pedras
Nuth Lounge
Concert Halls
Cidade da Música
Citibank Hall
HSBC Arena

Further Afield

Arts/Cultural Centres
Casa da Cultura
Bars
Bar Tom Maior
Taberna Dom Beto
Cinemas and Theatres
Gran Cine Bardot
Teatro Espaço
Clubs and Dancehalls
Chez Michou
Privilege

Entertainment A–Z

00

www.00site.com.br

This slick modern cocktail bar (whose name is pronounced 'Zero Zero') has the local elite dancing to live and DJ house music in a romantic candlelit lounge. A small garden at the back provides a quieter corner.

🔢 A11 ✉ Avenida Padre Leonel Franca 240, Gávea ☎ 2540 8041 🕐 Daily from 8.30pm 🚌 571, 583, 593

ACADEMIA DA CACHAÇA

www.academiadacachaca.com.br

For those who want to get serious about their cachaça, this is a serious, no-frills bar, with some 100 brands to choose from. It also serves regional Brazilian dishes (such as *vatapá carioquinha*—fish and seafood with passionfruit *farofa*). It's extremely popular, especially at weekends.

🔢 A12 ✉ Rua Conde Bernadotte 26G, Leblon ☎ 2529 2680 🕐 Tue–Sat noon–2am, Sun noon–1am 🚌 172, 173, 593

BAR D'HOTEL

www.marinaallsuites.com.br/allsuites/portugues/bar-hotel.asp

Enjoy exotic cocktails in this romantic bar overlooking the beach. Laidback DJ sounds attract a smart, young crowd; it livens up only after 11.

🔢 B12 ✉ Avenida Delfim Moreira 696, Leblon ☎ 2172 1100 🕐 Daily 7pm–2am 🚌 175, 177, 382

BAR DA LADEIRA

www.matrizonline.com.br

Listen to authentic live samba in a traditional *boteco* bar (with great chilled beer and snacks). Part of the multi-faceted Matriz group,

it's more relaxed than most of Lapa's heaving clubs, and is in a converted mansion typical of the area.

🔢 G3 ✉ Rua Evaristo da Veiga 149, Lapa ☎ 2226 9691 🕐 Shows: Tue–Sat 10pm, Sun 6pm 🚇 Carioca

BAR TOM MAIOR

Musicians play *choro* and *chorinho* (romantic ballads accompanied by the guitar and *cavaquinho*) at this atmospheric little bar spilling out onto the pavement.

🔢 Map, ▷ 110 ✉ Rua Luís de Almeida Pinto 13, Conservatória, Vale do Café ☎ (24) 2438 1460 🕐 Daily 10am until late (music Fri–Sat evening and Sun lunch)

BARETTO LONDRA

www.fasano.com.br

This fashionable bar is themed on Fasano-owner Rogerio Fasano's favourite city, London, and is decorated with UK rock album covers. DJs play house and occasional rock (if Rogerio ever gets his way).

🔢 D12 ✉ Hotel Fasano, Avenida Vieira Souto 80 ☎ 3202 4000 🕐 Mon–Sat from 7pm 🚇 Ipanema/General Osório

---

SURF BUS

If you're not staying in Barra, the Surf Bus is a handy way of getting to its beaches. Specially equipped for surf dudes, the 30-seater bus has storage space for surf boards, an on-board bar, pounding sound system and DVD player. Buses from Largo do Machado (Catete) go to Prainha, at the far end of Barra, via Copacabana, Ipanema and Leblon; the journey time is 1.5 hours (☎ 8702 2837/2539 7555; www.surfbus.com.br 🕐 Daily 7, 10, 1 and 4, returning 8.30, 11.30, 2.30 and 5.30 💳 R$4 one-way).

The Cidade da Música

BARONNETI

www.baronneti.com.br

One of Ipanema's top and trendiest clubs plays a wide range of music, from house to *baile funk*.
⊞ C12 ✉ Rua Barão da Torre 354, Ipanema ☎ 2247 9100 ◉ Fri–Sat from 10pm ◙ Ipanema/General Osório

BIP BIP

A packed crowd of loyal *cariocas* fills this tiny bar, which plays sublime live samba and *pagode*.
⊞ E11 ✉ Rua Almirante Goncalves 50, Copacabana ☎ 2267 9696 ◉ Daily 6.30pm–1am ◙ Cantagalo ◙ 154, 433, 523

BOOX

www.boox.com.br

In this smart club upstairs in a self-styled 'lounge-cuisine' restaurant, DJs and live bands play a smooth mix of house and jazz.
⊞ C12 ✉ Rua Barão da Torre 368, Ipanema ☎ 7890 9241 ◉ Wed–Sat from 8pm ◙ Ipanema/General Osório

OPENING HOURS

Most nightclubs in Rio start and end very late, not getting lively until after 10pm and carrying on through to the wee hours.

BUNKER 94

This massively popular DJ club packs in a lively crowd. There's acid rock, funk, house, samba and more, on three dance floors, plus a quiet lounge.
⊞ E12 ✉ Rua Raul Pompeia 94, Copacabana ☎ 3813 0300 ◉ Daily 11pm–4am ◙ Ipanema/General Osório

CARIOCA DA GEMA

www.barcariocadagema.com.br

There's live samba every night at this wonderful old-fashioned bar, which is particularly popular on Mondays, when most other clubs are closed.
⊞ F3 ✉ Avenida Mem de Sá 79, Lapa ☎ 2221 0043 ◉ Mon–Fri 7pm–late, Sat 9pm–late, Sun 8pm–late ◙ 433, 464, 572

CASA DA CULTURA

www.casadaculturaparaty.org.br

Paraty's municipal arts centre has a lively programme of cinema, art exhibitions, music and drama and is also one of the main bases for FLIP—Paraty's renowned International Literary Festival. There's an excellent little bookshop and café.
⊞ Map, ▷ 110 ✉ Rua Dona Geralda 177, Paraty ☎ (24) 3371 2325 ◉ Wed–Mon 10–6.30

CASTELO DAS PEDRAS

www.castelodaspedras.com.br

Tour company Be a Local runs group visits to this no-frills, hot-and-heaving *baile funk* club in the Favela das Pedras. It's the safest way to experience this upbeat, genuinely local club.
⊞ Map, ▷ 105 d4 ✉ Avenida das Américas 700, Barra da Tijuca ◉ Sun from 10pm ◙ Transport provided by Be a Local, tel 9643 0366

CENTRO CULTURAL CASA ROSA

www.casarosa.com.br

High on a Laranjeiras hillside, this huge pink house with a saucy past as a high society 'cabaret' is now a lively cultural centre with a booming reputation. Daytime sees a mixed programme, from poetry to book readings. Evening concerts span jazz to samba-rock, reggae and dub groove sounds.

🎫 E6 ✉ Rua Alice 550, Laranjeiras
☎ 2557 2562 🕐 Thu–Sun shows from 10pm 🚇 Largo do Machado 🚌 406, 407

CHEZ MICHOU

www.chezmichou.com.br

Nominally a crêperie, and a pretty good one at that, Chez Michou's biggest attraction for its hip young clientele is its nightclub. DJs play house music on Wednesdays from 11pm, continuing loud and long into the night. It also hosts theatre, cinema and other art events.

🎫 Map, ▷ 111 ✉ Avenida José Bento Ribeiro Dantas 90, Búzios ☎ (22) 2623 2169 🕐 Daily noon–late

CIDADE DA MÚSICA

This angular modern cultural complex is the home of the Brazilian Symphony Orchestra. The main concert hall seats 1,800, and there are four cinema screens, a restaurant, bar and shops.

🎫 Map, ▷ 105 c4 ✉ Avenida Ayrton Senna, Barra da Tijuca ☎ 2431 6120
🚌 179, 523

CINE SANTA TERESA

www.cinesanta.com.br

A locally loved 60-seat cinema, Cine Santa Teresa also holds art exhibitions and charity campaigns for *favela* children. There's also

a small coffee bar in the foyer.

🎫 F4 ✉ Largo dos Guimarães, Santa Teresa ☎ 2222 0203 🕐 Café: daily 10–10. Cinema: 4 screenings daily from 3pm
🚇 Largo dos Guimarães

CIRCO VOADOR

www.circovoador.com.br

This white marquee next to the Arcos da Lapa pulsates through the night with live rock, rap, reggae and samba. It also runs a popular monthly *baile funk* night. Daytime courses include afro-dance, drumming and *capoeira*.

🎫 F3 ✉ Rua dos Arcos, Lapa ☎ 2533 0354 🕐 Fri–Sun evenings 🚇 Carioca

CITIBANK HALL

www.citibankhall.com.br

Top Brazilian and international stars appear at this giant entertainment venue, as well as stage shows such as *Miss Saigon*.

🎫 Map, ▷ 105 c4 ✉ Avenida Ayrton Senna 3000, Barra da Tijuca ☎ 0300 789 6846 🚌 175, 177, 179

CLUBE DOS DEMOCRÁTICOS

www.clubedosdemocraticos.com.br

Founded in 1867, this stately old social club has a reputation for some of Rio's best live samba and

● Several festivals take place in and around Búzios each year. June sees the *Rio das Ostras Jazz e Blues* festival (www.riodasostrasjazzeblues.com). Now based in a resort further up the coast, the festival is rated the best of its kind in Brazil. Mid-October sees the *Búzios Gastronomy Festival* (www.redeturis.org), and November has the *Búzios Film Festival* (www.buzioscinefestival.org.br).

● The *Festival Vale do Café* (www.festival valedocafe.com) is the region's main music event, held in the second half of July and attracting big crowds. Brazilian music is performed in the *fazendas*, churches and squares of Vassouras, Valença and other towns in the valley.

forró acts. Despite its formal appearance, the atmosphere here gets pretty lively late into the night.
🕀 F3 ✉ Rua Riachuelo 91–93, Lapa ☎ 2252 4611 ⏱ Thu–Sat 10pm–late, Sun 8pm–late 🚇 Glória

DEVASSA
This is the original bar of a success-ful microbrewery with other outlets around the city. Its brews offer a refreshing alternative to lager; its long wooden tables are packed with appreciative locals.
🕀 A12 ✉ Avenida General San Martin 1241, Leblon ☎ 2259 8271 ⏱ Daily until late 🚌 432, 435, 593

ELITE
A lively *gafieira* (dance hall) in a venerable 19th-century building, Elite has hosted a pedigree line-up since the 1930s and attracts a slightly older and smarter crowd.
🕀 E3 ✉ Rua Frei Caneca 4 ☎ 2232 3217 ⏱ Fri 9pm–late, Sun 10pm–late 🚇 Central (safer by taxi)

ESTUDANTINA
It may have age-worn decor, but this traditional *gafieira* packs in locals and tourists alike. There's ballroom dancing, from samba to salsa, on Wednesday and Saturday (samba dance classes are available); with live samba, *choro* and jazz on Friday.
🕀 F3 ✉ Praca Tiradentes 79 ☎ 2232 1149 ⏱ Wed 7pm–1am, Fri 8pm–1pm, Sat 10pm–2am 🚇 Presidente Vargas

FUNDIÇÃO PROGRESSO
www.fundicao.org
This concert hall next to Circo Voador hosts big-name bands and a variety of arts events and shows.
🕀 F3 ✉ Rua dos Arcos, Lapa ☎ 2220 5070 🚇 Cinelândia

GAROTA DE IPANEMA
The bar where Tom Jobim and Vinicius de Moraes wrote the world's most famous bossa-nova song is touristy now, but worth a visit for a cool beer as you watch today's beautiful people pass by.
🕀 D12 ✉ Rua Vinicius de Moraes 49A, Ipanema ☎ 2523 3787 ⏱ Daily noon–2am 🚇 Ipanema/General Osório

GRAN CINE BARDOT
www.viladomar.com/cinebardot/
This is the only cinema in Búzios, and venue of the film festival. It screens the latest Brazilian and international movies.
🕀 Map, ▷ 111 ✉ Travessa dos Pescadores 88, Búzios ☎ (22) 2623 1466 ⏱ Thu–Sun

HSBC ARENA
www.hsbcarena.com.br
This multi-purpose stadium hosts Rio's major basketball games and also stages concerts.

⊞ Map, ▷ 104 c4 ✉ Avenida Embaixador Abelardo Bueno 3401, Barra da Tijuca ☎ 3035 5200 🚌 268

JOBI

Jobi is a small but popular late-night bar that has been going since 1953. It's great for a tasty sandwich after a heavy night's clubbing.

⊞ A12 ✉ Avenida Ataulfo de Paiva 1166, Loja B, Leblon ☎ 2274 0547 🕐 Mon–Fri 9am–4am, Sat–Sun 9am–dawn 🚌 177, 577

MELT

www.meltbar.com.br

This big club (pronounced 'Melch') attracts a more mixed following than the typical Leblon elite scene. There's a good line-up of bands and DJs, with hip hop, MPB, pop, rock and samba.

⊞ A12 ✉ Rua Rita Ludolf 47, Leblon ☎ 2249 9309 🕐 Fri–Sun 10pm–late 🚌 574, 591, 593

MISTURA FINA

A long-standing, traditional club on the Copacabana-Ipanema border, Mistura Fina has a piano bar and restaurant. It hosts live acts with roots in 1960s bossa nova.

⊞ E12 ✉ Avenida Rainha Elizabeth 770, Ipanema ☎ 2523 1703 🕐 Fri–Sun 11pm–late 🚇 Ipanema/General Osório

NUTH LOUNGE

www.nuth.com.br

A wide range of music keeps Barra's smart young clubbers going

until dawn at Nuth Lounge—the more laidback partner to Lagoa's Nuth Club—with anything from hip hop to samba and jazz, via electronica and techno. There are resident DJs, bands, a romantic open-air lounge and an upstairs restaurant. Come before 10pm or expect a two-hour wait.

⊞ Map, ▷ 105 d4 ✉ Avenida Armando Lombardi 999, Barra da Tijuca ☎ 3153 8595 🕐 Nightly 9pm–5am 🚌 179, 523

OI FUTURO IPANEMA

www.oifuturo.org.br

See live bands in an intimate venue, part of Oi Futuro cultural institute (with a theatre in Flamengo), which promotes innovative talent.

⊞ D12 ✉ Rua Visconde de Pirajá 54, Ipanema 🕐 Hours vary 🚇 Ipanema/ General Osório

PLATAFORMA 1

www.plataforma.com

This over-the-top but fun samba show has a restaurant and another

ENTERTAINMENT

KIOSKS

The 20 or so kiosks around Lagoa Rodrigo de Freitas are all independently run. As well as serving anything from Middle Eastern to Japanese snacks, many also put on live music in the evenings, particularly those on the south side, near the skate park. Check www.lagoarodrigodefreitas. com.br for details.

stage in Bar do Tom. It occasionally features famous artists.
⊞ B11 ⊠ Rua Adalberto Ferreira 32, Leblon ☎ 2274 4022 ⊙ Daily 10–11.30pm 🚌 464 from Leblon

PRIVILEGE

www.privilegenet.com.br
In a chic resort like Búzios, this nightclub attracts the greatest quantity of celebs and other rich and beautiful folk. It's big enough for plenty of normal funseekers too, with a capacity of 1,200, spread over two dance floors, four bars and several restaurants and lounge areas. DJs play everything from rock'n'roll to techno house.
⊞ Map, ▷ 111 ⊠ Avenida José

Bento Ribeiro Dantas 550, Búzios ☎ (22) 2623 0150 ⊙ Hours vary

RIO SCENARIUM

www.rioscenarium.com.br
Part music club, part antiques store, Rio Scenarium is in a magical, rambling old warehouse, eccentrically decorated with ephemera, from a vintage American car to suits of armour. Most of all, though, this is a great place to hear top-quality live samba, *forró, choro* and MPB.
⊞ F3 ⊠ Rua do Lavradio 20, Lapa ☎ 3147 9005 ⊙ Tue–Thu 6.30pm–late, Fri 7–late, Sat–Sun 8–late 🚌 158, 394

SALA CECÍLIA MEIRELES

www.salaceciliameireles.com.br
An elegant 19th-century former hotel is now a leading classical auditorium, with chamber music and occasional jazz concerts.
⊞ F4 ⊠ Largo da Lapa 47, Lapa ☎ 2332 9176 🚇 Cinelândia

O SEMENTE

Tucked under one of the archways of the Arcos da Lapa, this little bar

The Centro Cultural Oi Futuro promotes innovative talent

Outside Circo Voador nightclub in Lapa

punches above its weight as home of many top local musicians, with great improvised jamming sessions. Hear jazz, samba and other Latin American styles.

🔲 F3 ⊠ Rua Joaquim Silva 138, Lapa ☎ 2509 3591 🕐 Sun–Thu, from 9.30pm 🚇 Glória

TABERNA DOM BETO

Beto's bar is one of Conservatória's main hubs for hearing *choro*, very popular in this area, with its history of *seresta* minstrels strolling the streets. There's also a restaurant, specializing in grilled cod.

🔲 Map, ▷ 110 ⊠ Rua Dr Luiz Almeida Pinto 67, Conservatória, Vale do Café ☎ (24) 2438 1431 🕐 Fri–Sat 5pm–late

TEATRO ESPAÇO

www.ecparaty.org.br

The show at this highly acclaimed puppet theatre gives a bawdy but touching view of Brazilians at home, work and play: no words, just music, dance and amazingly lifelike movement. No under-15s.

🔲 Map, ▷ 110 ⊠ Rua Dona Geralda 327, Paraty ☎ (24) 3371 1575 🕐 Wed, Sat 9pm

THEATRO MUNICIPAL

www.theatromunicipal.rj.gov.br

This magnificently ornate 19th-century belle époque-style theatre is home of the Municipal Theatre Symphony Orchestra, with a programme of classical concerts, including a special Christmas event, opera and ballet.

🔲 G3 ⊠ Praça Floriano ☎ 2332 9195 🚇 Cinelândia

UP

A fresh new addition to Copacabana's entertainment scene, Up has eclectic retro decor

TIP

For details of what's on in Lapa, visit Lá na Lapa: www.lanalapa.com.br.

and attracts a young crowd. Its DJs play hip hop on Fridays and a mix of styles other nights.

🔲 E11 ⊠ Avenida Nossa Senhora de Copacabana 1144, Copacabana 🕐 Thu–Sun 10pm–late 🚇 Cantagalo

VERÃO DO MORRO

www.veraodomorro.com.br

Verão do Morro is a season of samba shows, cinema and live music during the weeks leading up to Carnaval. It's a great setting in an amphitheatre halfway up Sugarloaf mountain.

🔲 H8 ⊠ Avenida Pasteur 520, Urca ☎ 2461 2700 🕐 Fri–Sun 10.30pm–late 🚌 511, 512

THE WEEK

www.theweek.com.br

Rio's biggest gay club has an outdoor swimming pool. Two dance floors play electro and tribal house, funk and retro dance music; there are also bands and entertainment.

🔲 F1 ⊠ Rua Sacadura Cabral 150, Saúde ☎ 2253 1020 🕐 Mon–Sat 11pm–late 🚇 Central (safer by taxi)

OPEN DOORS

For one week every July, artists in Santa Teresa hold the *Portas Abertas* 'Open Doors' event, with dozens of studios showing their latest artworks. Live music and entertainment spill out of bars onto the streets, creating a party atmosphere. Restaurants join in the fun, too, cooking up special gastronomic menus. For more information ☎ 2507 5352; www.artedeportasabertas.com.br.

Eat

There are places to eat across the city to suit all tastes and budgets. In this section establishments are listed alphabetically.

EAT

Introduction

Cariocas love to eat out. Whole families spend hours socializing late into the night. With its tropical climate and beach culture, Rio has many open-air restaurants. Dress code in even the smartest establishments is distinctly casual, though stylish locals dress up fashionably for special occasions.

What to Eat

Dining in Rio is a gastronomic treat, reflecting the city's diverse cultural influences. Options include French, Middle Eastern, Asian, Italian and Portuguese restaurants. Seafood is excellent, with regional Amazonian cuisine and Afro-Brazilian dishes from the northeast, specializing in spicy sauces with coconut milk and palm oil. For carnivores, *churrascarias* are all-you-can-eat barbecues, where waiters brandish giant skewers spiked with succulent chunks of meat. *Por kilo* restaurants are self-service cafeterias where you pay by the weight of your chosen dishes. The nearest thing to a national dish is the *feijoada*—a hearty meat-and-beans stew accompanied by *farofa* (toasted ground manioc), rice, cabbage and orange slices, with a cachaça to help digest. Rustic and filling Minas Gerais cuisine, from the landlocked state tucked behind Rio, includes hearty stews of pork and beans.

Where to Eat

Copacabana has the biggest concentration of eateries. Lapa's bustling backstreets are lined with funky late-night snack bars. Santa Teresa's leafy squares favour exotic upmarket joints, while Ipanema, Lagoa and Leblon have top-ranked and similarly priced fine-dining options.

WHEN TO EAT

Breakfast usually starts relatively late, from around 8am. Lunch is the main meal of the day, served from midday until about 3pm. Dinner—a lighter meal—starts after 9pm.

From top: The famous Porcão Rio's restaurant; chefs at Roberta Sudbrack; a waiter carving beef at Porcão Rio's; a traditional seafood dish

Directory

Downtown and Northern Rio

Cafés and Bars
Armazém Senado
Bar Luiz
Bistro the Line
Confeitaria Colombo
Meat Feasts
Beduíno
Seafood
Albamar
Margutta Cittá
Vegetarian
Tempeh

Baia de Guanabara

Brazilian
Lamas
Yorubá
European
Miam Miam
Meat Feasts
Porcão Rio's
Por Kilo Restaurants
Praia Vermelha Restaurante

Copacabana, Ipanema and Leblon

Cafés and Bars
Bracarense
Café do Lage
Cervantes
Juice Co
Fusion
Le Pré Catelan
Roberta Sudbrack
Meat Feasts
Arab da Lagoa
Casa da Feijoada
Seafood
Fasano al Mare
Siri Mole & Cia

Vegetarian
Celeiro
Líquido
Mil Frutas
Vegetariano Social Clube

The Hills

Brazilian
Os Esquilos
Cafés and Bars
Bar do Mineiro
Belmonte
Mangue Seco Cachacaria
European
Adega do Pimenta
Fusion
Aprazivel
Espírito Santa
Santa Arte
Seafood
Sobrenatural

Beach Suburbs

Cafés and Bars
Barraca do Pepê
European
Beco do Alemão
Meat Feasts
Tourão
Seafood
Point de Grumari
Skunna
Vegetarian
Delírio Tropical

Further Afield

Brazilian
Arcadia Bistrô Imperatriz
Bordeaux Vinhos & Cia
A Mineira
Pousada da Alcobaca

Cafés and Bars
Chocolate Katz
European
Brigitta's
Oliveiras da Serra
Punto di Vino
Fusion
Sawasdee
Meat Feasts
Porcão Niterói
Por Kilo Restaurants
Boom
Familia Paludo
Seafood
Banana da Terra
Bar dos Pescadores

EAT

PRICES

Prices are approximate, based on a three-course meal for one person.

$$$$	over R$105
$$$	R$70–R$105
$$	R$35–R$70
$	under R$35

ADEGA DO PIMENTA $$

www.adegadopimenta.com.br

This restaurant serves German specialities, including hearty sauerkraut and sausages, and a wide range of imported bottled beers. At weekends you can enjoy a German-style *feijoada*.

➕ F4 ☒ Rua Almirante Alexandrino 296, Santa Teresa ☎ 2224 7554 ⓦ Daily lunch and dinner 🚋 Tram to Largo dos Guimarães

ALBAMAR $$$

www.albamar.com.br

This traditional gourmet restaurant is in the last remaining tower of the old Municipal Market building. It's a great dockside setting, with views of the bay and Ilha Fiscal. The seafood is very good; specials include whiting baked with prawns and mussels in white wine, and *bolinhos de bacalhau* (cod balls). Dapper elderly waiters add to the distinguished ambience.

➕ H2 ☒ Praça Marechal Âncora 184–186, Centro ☎ 2240 8378 ⓦ Mon–Fri lunch (11.30–6) 🚇 Carioca

APRAZÍVEL $$$

www.aprazivel.com.br

Sample excellent Minas Gerais cuisine with a French twist, such as *galinhada caipira*—chicken risotto with plantain, beans and *farofa*.

There are palm-roofed terraces with wonderful views across the city centre, and occasional Sunday afternoon live jazz.

➕ F5 ☒ Rua Aprazível 62, Santa Teresa ☎ 3508 9174 ⓦ Tue–Sat lunch and dinner, Sun and hols lunch (12–7) 🚋 Tram to Largo dos Guimarães

ARAB DA LAGOA $$

In a lovely spot by the lake shore, this place serves tasty couscous salads, *kibe* (spicy minced lamb rissoles), pizzas and Moroccan-style mezze. Many dishes are big enough for two. There's also live jazz in the evening, for a small cover charge.

➕ B10 ☒ Parque dos Patins, Avenida Borges de Medeiros, Lagoa ☎ 2540 0747 ⓦ Daily breakfast, lunch and dinner 🚌 128

ARCADIA BISTRÔ IMPERATRIZ $$

www.bistroimperatriz.com.br

Delightfully situated in the grounds of the Imperial Palace, Arcadia Bistrô Imperatriz is ideal for after-noon tea, with home-made cakes and pastries. It also serves good steaks, fish, risottos and seafood.

➕ Map, ▷ 111 ☒ Museu Imperial, Rua do Imperatriz 220, Petrópolis ☎ (24) 2231 1188 ⓦ Tue–Sun breakfast, lunch, dinner

ARMAZÉM SENADO $

In a converted warehouse, this lively street-corner bar has been in business since 1907, and serves a range of chilled beers, snacks and cold cuts. There's live music on the first Saturday of the month for the nearby antiques fair, the Feira do Rio Antigo (▷ 123, panel).

➕ F3 ☒ Avenida Gomes Freire 256, Centro/Lapa ☎ 2509 7201 ⓦ Mon–Sat breakfast, lunch and dinner 🚇 Carioca

BANANA DA TERRA $$$

One of the best restaurants in Paraty specializes in local *Caiçara*-style seafood, with plantain a key ingredient for mains as well as desserts. Try the seafood risotto, or stuffed squid in coconut milk.
🗺 Map, ▷ 110 ✉ Rua Dr Samuel Costa 198, Paraty ☎ (024) 3371 1725
🕓 Wed–Mon lunch and dinner

BAR LUIZ $$

www.barluiz.com.br
A *carioca* favourite, this art deco bar has been here since 1927. It specializes in German-style sausages and potato salad, washed down with ice-cold beer. There's a German set lunch for two (*Alemão Completo*) on Saturdays.
🗺 G3 ✉ Rua da Carioca 39, Centro
☎ 2262 6900 🕓 Mon–Sat lunch and dinner 🚇 Carioca

BAR DO MINEIRO $$

This longstanding locals' bar, decorated with antiques and artworks, specializes in Mineira cuisine (big on rich meat stews) and excellent *feijoada* on Saturdays.
🗺 F4 ✉ Rua Paschoal Carlos Magno 99, Santa Teresa ☎ 2508 8580 🕓 Tue–Sun lunch and dinner 🚋 Tram to Largo dos Guimarães

BAR DOS PESCADORES $$

www.bardospescadores.com.br
Enjoy delicious fresh fish, served on sizzling platters big enough for two. This is the best of a cluster of beachside restaurants on a tree-shaded courtyard by the Manguinhos fish market. Starters include crab, prawn and cheese pasties—wonderful with a dash of Tabasco sauce.
🗺 Map, ▷ 111 ✉ Avenida José Bento

ON A BUDGET

● On weekdays many places offer the good-value *cardápio executivo* set lunch, which is quick and freshly made.
● Many Middle Eastern restaurants and snack bars offer good-value set meals, particularly around the Saara market (▷ 121, panel) and on Rua Ouvidor and Rua do Rosário (🚇 Uruguaiana).

Ribeiro Dantas 85, Búzios ☎ (22) 2623 6785 🕓 Wed–Mon lunch and dinner

BARRACA DO PEPÊ $

www.pepe.com.br
There's a cult following for this beach snack bar, run by the widow of Pepê, a famous hang-glider, who was killed in a gliding accident in Japan. The snack bar serves tasty and healthy sandwiches, salads and snacks, as well as excellent smoothies, including Rio's health-food wonder-fruit, *açaí*.
🗺 Map, ▷ 105 d4 ✉ Quiosque 11, Avenida do Pepê, Barra da Tijuca ☎ 2433 1400 🕓 Daily breakfast, lunch and dinner 🚌 233, 524

BECO DO ALEMÃO $$

http://becodoalemao.com.br
Despite its unappealing location next to a service station, this is a very popular spot at weekend lunchtimes for its *por kilo* buffet. There's German cuisine on Tuesdays and Minas Gerais specialities on Thursdays.
🗺 Map, ▷ 105 d4 ✉ Avenida das Américas 1600, Barra da Tijuca ☎ 2493 9326 🕓 Mon–Sat lunch and dinner, Sun lunch (until 6.30) 🚌 175, 177, 524

BEDUÍNO $

Sample Middle Eastern specialities, including *kibe* (spicy minced lamb

Copacabana and Ipanema have Rio's highest concentration and widest variety of eateries; prices tend to rise the closer you get to the beach, not always matched by better food. It's worth exploring side streets a few blocks inland, where you might find a hidden local favourite. Lagoa is the place to go if you fancy a romantic lakeside meal. Further into the neighbourhood and the adjacent Jardim Botânico district are several clusters of upmarket restaurants, especially around Rua J. J. Seabra and Rua Pacheco Leão.

rissole), *esfiha de frango* (chicken pasty), *taboule* (bulgar-wheat salad), salads and pasta. There's a good-value set meal for two.

➕ G3 ✉ Avenida Presidente Wilson 1234, Centro ☎ 2524 5142 🕐 Mon–Fri breakfast, lunch and dinner, Sat breakfast and lunch (until 5) 🚇 Cinelândia

BELMONTE $$

www.botecobelmonte.com.br

This *boteco* bar is famous for its bohemian clientele and the ice-chilled chopp draft beer. The menu focuses on Brazilian steak dishes, plus *feijoada* on Saturday. It's just around the corner from Rua do Lavradio, with its antiques market Feira do Rio Antigo (▷ 123, panel).

➕ F3 ✉ Avenida Mem de Sá, Lapa 🕐 Tue–Sun lunch and dinner 🚌 433, 464, 572

BISTRO THE LINE $$

Inside the Casa França Brasil, with tables on a peaceful patio, this bistro serves good snacks, a buffet lunch and yummy cakes.

➕ G2 ✉ Rua Visconde de Itaborai ☎ 2233 3571 🕐 Daily breakfast, lunch and dinner (10–8) 🚌 132

BOOM $$–$$$

www.boombuzios.com.br

Widely considered the best *por kilo* restaurant in Búzios, Boom is also one of the first, opening in 1995. Its gourmet buffet offers a global range of dishes, from Minas Gerais bean soup to Japanese sushi. There's also an à la carte menu ($$$) and cocktail bar. The stylish modern building has a spacious balcony lounge area.

➕ Map, ▷ 111 ✉ Rua Manoel Turibio de Farias, Búzios ☎ (22) 2623 6254 🕐 Daily lunch and dinner

BORDEAUX VINHOS & CIA $$

www.bordeauxvinhos.com.br

This is a romantic setting, in the old coach house of the Casa da Ipiranga, one of Petrópolis' stately mansions. Enjoy Brazilian and international cuisine, with a huge cellar of 1,500 wines.

➕ Map, ▷ 111 ✉ Avenida Ipiranga 716, Petrópolis ☎ (24) 2242 5711 🕐 Daily lunch and dinner (until 7 on Sun)

BRACARENSE $

www.bracarense.com.br

One of Rio's great *boteco* bars serves good-value snacks and ice-cold beer to its loyal local clientele. It's packed on sunny weekends with people heading to and from the beach, a few blocks away.

➕ B12 ✉ Rua José Linhares 85, Loja B, Leblon ☎ 2294 3549 🕐 Daily lunch and dinner 🚌 175, 177, 583

BRIGITTA'S $$

www.brigittas.com.br

The restaurant of Czech-born Brigitta Anders serves genuine goulash, alongside exotic dishes such as African-style ostrich filet and Russian-style steak tartare. It has a lovely seafront location, as well as a guest house. Occasionally there's live music.

🔲 Map, ▷ 111 ✉ Rua das Pedras 131, Búzios ☎ (22) 2623 2940 🕐 Daily lunch and dinner

CAFÉ DO LAGE $$

Possibly the most picturesque café in Rio, here you sit at outdoor tables in a neoclassical atrium by a pond next to the Parque Lage. It serves decent cakes, sandwiches and light lunches.

🔲 C9 ✉ Rua Jardim Botânico 414, Jardim Botânico ☎ 2226 8125 🕐 Mon–Fri breakfast, lunch and dinner, Sat–Sun breakfast and lunch 🚌 170, 172, 571

CASA DA FEIJOADA $$$

www.cozinhatipica.com.br

This small restaurant serves some of the best *feijoada* in Rio. You can savour huge portions at reasonable prices, washed down with a knockout *batida* (cachaça and fruit cocktail).

🔲 D12 ✉ Rua Prudente de Morais 10 ☎ 2247 2776 🕐 Daily lunch and dinner 🚌 570, 572

CELEIRO $$

This tiny but frequently award-winning vegetarian restaurant (with some meat dishes) offers *por kilo* or menu service. The buffet has crisp salads, light quiches and wholesome soups. Menu highlights include Thai stir-fry with couscous, and squash soufflé with vegetable risotto. It gets very crowded at lunchtimes.

🔲 A12 ✉ Rua Dias Ferreira 199, Leblon ☎ 2274 7843 🕐 Daily breakfast and lunch 🚌 433, 512

CERVANTES $

Considered by many to make the best sandwiches in Rio, Cervantes bar and nearby restaurant regularly have customers queuing down the street for their high stacks of meat, melted cheese, fish and salads, enveloped in fresh crusty bread. You'll find snappy service, waiters with attitude and adoring *carioca* fans.

🔲 G9 ✉ Rua Barata Ribeiro 7 (bar), Avenida Prado Junior 335 (restaurant), Copacabana ☎ 2275 6147 🕐 Tue–Sun lunch and dinner 🚇 Cardeal Arcoverde

Lunch is the main meal of the day in Rio

Roberta Sudbrack restaurant

Ipanema is your best bet for vegetarian restaurants, which are otherwise rare in Brazil. *Por kilo* restaurants include a good range of fresh salads and vegetable dishes; and although the national dish, *feijoada*, is based on meat, it also comes with separate servings of rice, beans, cabbage and *farofa* (ground manioc flour—though check first it's not cooked with pieces of bacon in it!).

CHOCOLATE KATZ $

If you're looking for a pit-stop for coffee and cake, this is a great place. The deli café, in the old part of Petrópolis, has been making its own chocolates since 1953.
➕ Map, ▷ 111 ✉ Rua do Imperador 912, Petrópolis ☎ (24) 2231 1191 ◉ Daily breakfast and lunch

CONFEITARIA COLOMBO $$

www.confeitariacolombo.com.br
Rio's most elegant and stately art nouveau tea house has stained-glass windows, huge mirrors, brass and wrought ironwork. Choose from delicious sandwiches, snacks, cakes and a good-value buffet-lunch specializing in Spanish and Portuguese dishes.
➕ G2 ✉ Rua Gonçalves Dias 32–36, Centro ☎ 2505 1500 ◉ Mon–Fri breakfast, lunch and dinner (9–8), Sat breakfast and lunch (9–5) 🚇 Carioca

DELÍRIO TROPICAL $

www.delirio.com.br
Healthy salads and tempting puddings are the highlights of this self-service buffet restaurant in the huge Barra Shopping mall (▷ 119). There's a wide range of cheeses—not often a speciality in Rio—as well as a choice of quiches and savoury crêpes.
➕ Map, ▷ 105 c4 ✉ Avenida das Américas 4666, Barra ☎ 3089 1170 ◉ Daily lunch and dinner 🚌 175, 177

ESPÍRITO SANTA $$$

www.espiritosanta.com.br
Manaus-born Natacha Fink serves up a gloriously imaginative menu, drawing largely on fish, fruits and vegetables from the Amazon, with a strong sustainability ethos. Try the *juma—tambaqui* fish marinated in lime and mint and served with caramelized grilled pineapple; or the *mujica de piraña* —a snappy fish soup. Espírito Santa is one of the city's finest and most eco-conscious restaurants.
➕ F4 ✉ Rua Almirante Alexandrino 264, Santa Teresa ☎ 2508 7095 ◉ Daily lunch and dinner 🚋 Tram to Largo dos Guimarães ❓ Occasional live music at weekends

OS ESQUILOS $$$

www.osesquilos.com.br
Treat yourself if you've just scaled Pico da Tijuca, or make a special trip to Tijuca National Park to eat at this delightful rustic restaurant in manicured grounds. The house (1852) has open beams, wooden flooring and a log fire in winter. Specialities include meat or cheese fondue, salmon with passion fruit, and filet mignon with sweet potato rosti. There's *feijoada* on Saturday and Sunday.
➕ A8 ✉ Estrada Barão d'Escragnolle, Floresta da Tijuca ☎ 2492 2197 ◉ Tue–Sun lunch (12–6) 🚕 Taxi

FAMILIA PALUDO $–$$

www.familiapaludo.com.br
This smart *por kilo* restaurant ($) on Icarai's seafront serves a wide range of meats, salads and grills in

the buffet, as well as *moqueca* (fish stew) and other specialities from northeastern Brazil. Adjoining Paludo Gourmet is also *por kilo*, with an à la carte option (*$$*).

🏠 Map, ▷ 111 ✉ Avenida Quintino Bocaiuva 247, Icaraí, Niterói ☎ 2715 3200 🕐 Daily lunch and dinner 🚌 Linha de Turismo bus to Icaraí

FASANO AL MARE $$$$

www.fasano.com.br

Sample gourmet Italian cuisine in Fasano's patio restaurant, enhanced by a sprinkle of celeb glamour. Dishes from Michelin three-star-winning chef Luca Gozzani include crayfish linguine, lobster risotto and fish ravioli.

🏠 D12 ✉ Hotel Fasano, Avenida Vieira Souto 80, Ipanema ☎ 3202 4000 🕐 Daily lunch and dinner 🚇 Ipanema/General Osório

JUICE CO $$

www.juiceco.com.br/2009

One of the best juice bars in Rio, this place mixes up interesting blends including Kill Gripe (Flu Killer, made of orange, mango and pineapple). There's also a modern menu including grilled fish. It's popular with Leblon's young elite.

🏠 A12 ✉ Rua General San Martin 889, Leblon ☎ 2294 0048 🕐 Daily lunch and dinner 🚌 132, 574

LAMAS $$

Founded in 1874, Lamas has stuck to what it does best, serving great meat dishes, such as *filé a Francesa* (steak with French-style fries and onions).

🏠 G6 ✉ Rua Marques do Abrantes 18, Flamengo ☎ 2556 0799 🕐 Daily breakfast, lunch and dinner (until 4am Fri–Sat) 🚇 Largo do Machado

---

COOKERY SCHOOL

Paraty's Academia de Cozinha is part restaurant, part cookery school, and a totally charming experience. Yara Castro Roberts teaches as she cooks a gourmet meal from a changing weekly regional cuisine, covering Amazonas, Cerrado, Bahia and Minas Gerais. Everyone then sits down to eat together as Yara and her US photographer husband Richard tell you about the region's culture and people (✉ Rua Dona Geralda 211, Paraty ☎ (24) 3371 6468 🕐 Tue–Sat ❓ Advanced booking only, 50 per cent deposit).

LÍQUIDO $$

This health juice bar overlooking Praça Nossa Senhora da Paz specializes in *dosas*—vegetarian stuffed crêpes (and some meat dishes, too). Best of all is an enticing selection of smoothly blended *batida* juices, organic Nepalese tea and caipirinhas made with organic cachaça.

🏠 C12 ✉ Rua Barão da Torre 398, Loja A, Ipanema ☎ 2267 6519 🕐 Daily lunch and dinner 🚌 132, 574

MANGUE SECO CACHAÇARIA $$

www.manguesecocachacaria.com.br/ms

Run by the owners of Rio Scenarium (▷ 136), this is one of the best places to eat in Lapa, with rustic decor and black-and-white photographs. The restaurant specializes in shellfish and fish dishes, with a tank of live crabs in the entranceway. The bar stocks more than 100 brands of cachaça, including high-quality brands from Paraty and Minas Gerais.

🏠 F3 ✉ Rua do Lavradio 23, Lapa ☎ 3852 1947 🕐 Mon–Sat lunch and dinner 🚇 Carioca

EAT

Outdoor eating on the Travessa do Comércio, in central Rio

MARGUTTA CITTÁ $$$

www.margutta.com.br/citta

This classy Italian restaurant, an offshoot of the original Margutta in Ipanema, has colourful decor and serves seafood risottos, grilled tilapia with prawns, and lamb, veal, chicken and steaks. Specials include *pesce alla Neroni*, oven-baked fish with polenta and rice.

⊞ G3 ⊠ Avenida Graca Aranha 1 (1st floor), Centro ☎ 2563 4091 ◉ Mon–Fri lunch ⊛ Cinelândia

MIAM MIAM $$$

www.miammiam.com.br

Chef Roberta Ciasca focuses on comfort food, but with imaginative twists, at this chic French restaurant with retro 1950s–70s decor. Dishes include grilled squid with lemon thai jelly, or beef stuffed with rocket, parmesan and herbs.

⊞ F9 ⊠ Rua General Góes Monteiro 34, Botafogo ☎ 2244 0125 ◉ Tue–Sun dinner ⊛ Botafogo

MIL FRUTAS $$

www.milfrutas.com.br

These ice creams are constantly voted the best in Rio. Mil Frutas creates more than 180 flavours using a dazzling range of Amazonian fruits, such as *graviola*, *pitanga* and *taperebá*.

⊞ B10 ⊠ Rua J.J. Seabra, Jardim Botânico (also branches in Ipanema, Leblon, Barra and São Conrado) ☎ 2511 2550 ◉ Daily breakfast, lunch, dinner ▣ 179, 571, 583

A MINEIRA $$

www.restauranteamineira.com.br

This cosy, rustic restaurant special-izes in Minas Gerais cuisine, which favours hearty stews, served with yucca, *farofa*, rice and beans. One of the best-value places in Niterói, it has menu or buffet options.

⊞ Map, ▷ 111 ⊠ Avenida Quintino Bocaiúva 353, Niterói ☎ (21) 2714 3676 ◉ Daily lunch and dinner ▣ Linha de Turismo bus to Icaraí

MALL EATERIES

Eating in shopping malls might not sound like an authentic Brazilian experience, but you can find an impressive range of choice under one roof, from snack bars to the full-blown gourmet experience.

OLIVEIRAS DA SERRA $$$

www.oliveirasdaserra.com.br

There are massive portions at this Portuguese country-style restaurant in the Vale dos Gourmets. Specialities include *bolinhos de bacalhau* (cod balls), *cabrito alentejana* (kid goat casserole) and excellent desserts.

🔲 Map, ▷ 111 ✉ Estrada Bernardo Coutinho 3575, Vale da Aldeia, Araras, Petrópolis ☎ (24) 2225 0520 🕙 Tue–Sun lunch and dinner

POINT DE GRUMARI $$

www.pointdegrumari.com.br

This superb seafood restaurant has a view over the vast Marambaia marshes and Sepetiba lagoon. More importantly, though, it serves delicious seafood, including mixed seafood chowder *(caldeirada)* and *moqueca de lagosta* (lobster in *dendê* oil and coconut milk). There's live music at weekends.

🔲 Map, ▷ 104 a5 ✉ Estrada do Grumari 710, Grumari ☎ 2410 1434 🕙 Daily lunch and dinner (until 6.30) 🚌 Taxi

PORÇÃO NITERÓI $$

www.porcao.com.br

Porção Niterói is an offshoot of the famous *churrascaria* Porção Rio's (▷ below). The food is just as good but half the price of the original.

🔲 Map, ▷ 111 ✉ Avenida Quintino Bocaiúva 151, Icaraí, Niterói ☎ 3461 7080 🕙 Daily lunch and dinner 🚌 Linha de Turismo bus to Icaraí

PORÇÃO RIO'S $$$

www.porcao.com.br

Rio's most famous all-you-can-eat *churrascaria* restaurant has waiters brandishing huge skewers loaded with steak, sausages and chicken.

WHERE TO GO

For a livelier night, Lapa is the place to go, though the food usually plays second fiddle to the music. Santa Teresa's gourmet restaurants offer a romantic scene; many places have leafy terraces with superb views over the city centre, very romantic on a starry night.

It's a magnet for meat-lovers. The Niterói branch (▷ this page) is just as good at half the price.

🔲 G6 ✉ Avenida Infante Dom Henrique, Aterro do Flamengo ☎ 3461 9020 🕙 Daily lunch and dinner 🚇 Flamengo then a taxi

POUSADA DA ALCOBAÇA $$

www.pousadadaalcobaca.com.br

Renowned local chef Dona Laura Góes runs this restaurant, serving fine country cuisine in a cosy *pousada* in gorgeous grounds. The fresh fruit and vegetables come from the adjacent farm, and the fish, meat and dairy produce is locally sourced. The menu includes delicious steaks, seafood and chicken, with home-made desserts a particular speciality.

🔲 Map, ▷ 111 ✉ Rua Agostinho Goulão 298, Correias, Petrópolis ☎ (24) 2221 1240 🕙 Daily lunch and dinner

PRAIA VERMELHA RESTAURANTE $

There are great views over Praia Vermelha to Sugarloaf at this bright and airy *por kilo* restaurant. With an excellent selection of meat, fish, pasta and salads, it's popular with local families for Sunday lunch. There's also an adjoining pizzeria.

🔲 H9 ✉ Praça General Tibúrcio, Urca ☎ 2275 7292 🕙 Daily lunch and dinner 🚌 511, 512

EAT

LE PRÉ CATELAN $$$$

ww2.leprecatelan.com.br

Highly feted chef Roland Villard serves sumptuous French-fusion cuisine at the Sofitel hotel's glitzy restaurant. Standout dishes in his Amazonian Gastronomic Voyage include *pirarucu* fish mousse, served with a dried scale for a spoon. It's pricey but superb cuisine.

🔛 E12 ⊠ Avenida Atlântica 4240, Copacabana ☎ 2525 1160 ⚙ Daily lunch and dinner 🚇 Cardeal Arcoverde

PUNTO DI VINO $$

www.puntodivino.com

This smart Italian restaurant serves excellent steaks from Argentina, locally caught fish and superb home-made pasta, pizza and gnocchi. The wine list is impressive.

🔛 Map, ▷ 110 ⊠ Rua Marechal Deodoro 129, Praça da Matriz, Paraty ☎ (24) 3371 1348 ⚙ Daily lunch and dinner

ROBERTA SUDBRACK $$$$

www.robertasudbrack.com.br

The adventurous chef running this gastronomic hot spot has cooked for former Brazilian president Enrique Cardoso, as well as Prince Charles, Tony Blair and Fidel Castro. The 'Sudbrack Experience' is an artistically presented feast, with innovative dishes such as sweet potato tartare, shrimp and okra caviar, and crayfish with *chuchu* and peanut cream. It's sensational for a special occasion.

🔛 B10 ⊠ Rua Lineu de Paula Machado 916 ☎ 3874 0139 ⚙ Daily lunch and dinner 🚌 170, 172, 524

SANTA ARTE $$

Enjoy contemporary fusion cuisine in a bright and airy setting, with paintings on the walls by Selarón, of Lapa's mosaic steps fame (▷ 67). Specialities include Peruvian-style ceviche and Italian risottos, as well as Brazilian stews and steaks. Background world music completes the global feel.

🔛 F4 ⊠ Rua Paschoal Carlos Magno 103, Santa Teresa ☎ 2242 9366 ⚙ Tue–Sun lunch and dinner 🚋 Tram to Largo dos Guimarães

SAWASDEE $$

A rarity in Brazil: a Thai restaurant, using local fish, seafood and the best tropical ingredients to create its famously spicy but smooth dishes. Their soups are excellent, such as *po teak*—shrimp soup with squid, mussels, ginger, shitake mushrooms and basil. Or try the salmon ceviche with lemongrass. It's true fusion cuisine, combining Asia, Brazil and the Andes!

🔛 Map, ▷ 111 ⊠ Avenida Jose Bento Ribeiro Dantas 500, Orla Bardot, Búzios ☎ (22) 2623 4644 ⚙ Daily lunch and dinner

SIRI MOLE & CIA $$$

www.sirimole.com.br

Delicious Bahian cuisine is served here; try *bobó de camarão*

THE FRESHEST FISH

Rio's main fish market is the Mercado de Peixe São Pedro in Niterói's harbourside Portugal Pequeno. Ice-packed rows of stalls downstairs are filled with freshly caught fish and seafood, including giant, weird and wonderful species, such as the bright pink *olho de cão* (Dog's Eye fish). Upstairs are good-value, no-frills fish restaurants. You can buy your own fish downstairs and they will cook it for you (⊠ Avenida Visconde do Rio Branco 55, Niterói ⚙ Tue–Sat 6–6, Sun 6–noon).

(prawns with coconut milk and chilli peppers) or *casquinha de siri* (stuffed crab in the shell). There's a good-value lunch buffet on Fridays and Saturdays.

🔒 E12 ✉ Rua Francisco Otaviano 50, Copacabana ☎ 2267 0894 ⏰ Daily lunch and dinner 🚌 175, 177

SKUNNA $$

www.skunna.com.br

This seafood restaurant offers a novel twist to the traditional *feijoada*: Skunna's version is made with squid, octopus, prawns and mussels, with a chunk or two of Portuguese-style sausage to beef up the flavour. The huge dish is easily big enough for two. Other house specials include prawn bruschetta, ceviche and seafood terrine. There are good views from the air-conditioned patio.

🔒 Map, ▷ 104 a4 ✉ Estrada dos Bandeirantes 2363, Vargem Grande ☎ 2428 1213 ⏰ Tue–Sun lunch and dinner 🚕 Taxi

SOBRENATURAL $$$

Modern art brightens the dark wooden walls at this pretty little restaurant. The menu specializes in fish and seafood; try the *moqueca de bacalhau* (cod cooked in coconut milk and *dendê* oil), or *coco de surubim* (Amazonian river fish cooked in coconut milk), both dishes for two.

🔒 F4 ✉ Rua Almirante Alexandrino 432, Santa Teresa ☎ 2224 1003 ⏰ Daily lunch and dinner 🚋 Tram to Largo dos Guimarães

TEMPEH $

One of downtown's best vegetarian restaurants has a laidback feel, with New Age music. The cuisine includes paella, Indonesian and Thai curries, sushi and stroganoff. *Tempeh* (soya *feijoada*) is the speciality. There's a *por kilo* system Monday to Friday and a self-service buffet on Saturday.

🔒 G2 ✉ Rua Primeiro de Marco 24 (1st floor) ☎ 2294 5200 ⏰ Mon–Sat lunch 🚇 Uruguaiana

TOURÃO $$

www.tourao.com.br

A popular *churrascaria* restaurant, Tourão also has buffet alternatives for non-carnivores, including salads, sushi and Middle Eastern dishes. The inclusive *rodízio* barbecue is cheaper Monday to Friday after 6.30pm.

🔒 Map, ▷ 105 c4 ✉ Praça São Perpétuo 116, Barra ☎ 2493 4055 ⏰ Daily lunch and dinner 🚌 179, 523

VEGETARIANO SOCIAL CLUBE $

www.vegetarianosocialclube.com.br

There's an excellent-value buffet until 6pm at this chic but inexpensive vegetarian restaurant. Tofu pancake and mushroom risotto are among the options on the dinner menu.

🔒 B11 ✉ Rua Conde Bernadotte 26, Leblon ☎ 2294 5200 ⏰ Daily lunch and dinner 🚌 175, 464

YORUBÁ $$$

Yorubá serves great cuisine from northeastern Brazil: a delectable Afro-influenced blend of fish and shellfish cooked in coconut milk and *dendê* palm oil. Try *moqueca de siri* (spicy crab stew), and wash it down with a warming cachaça and ginger caipirinha.

🔒 F8 ✉ Rua Arnaldo Quintela 94, Botafogo ☎ 2541 9387 ⏰ Wed–Fri dinner, Sat–Sun lunch 🚇 Botafogo

Sleep

From high-rise luxury hotels with rooftop pools to colonial *pousadas* or funky boutique B&Bs, Rio offers a complete range of accommodation options. In this section establishments are listed alphabetically.

SLEEP

Introduction

As much of life in Rio revolves around the beach, most hotels are concentrated in Copacabana, Ipanema and Leblon, in the Zona Sul. Here are many of the most luxurious hotels, but also some budget hostels, the latter usually a few blocks inland. Downtown has fewer hotels but nearby Santa Teresa and Flamengo both have good-value places to stay.

Facilities
Most beachfront hotels in the Zona Sul have a pool, gym, restaurant, bar and WiFi. Farther along the coast, in São Conrado and Barra, are international chain hotels, some with tennis courts and typical resort facilities. They are also more likely to have family rooms or suites, though budget hostels often have larger rooms too, including bunk-bed dorms.

Further Afield
Búzios and Paraty have intimate boutique hotels and *pousadas* (inns, some in colonial villas). The Vale do Café has restored coffee plantation houses *(fazendas)*, with leisure facilities in sumptuous grounds (contact Preservale: www.preservale.com.br). Some of the hotels in Búzios are dotted around the peninsula, so a taxi or private transport will be needed.

Other Options
If you are staying for a week or longer, apartment rental may be more economical than a hotel. The tourist office website has listings: www.rioguiaoficial.com.br.

PRICES
Most beachside hotels charge a premium for rooms with a sea view, or for your own balcony. Room rates shoot up during Carnaval and the New Year. Most hotels include breakfast in the price of the room, usually a cold buffet including tropical fruits, cheese and cold meat.

Accommodation ranges from tranquil pousadas *(top) to trendy hotels such as Fasano (bottom). And some hotels offer glorious views*

SLEEP

Directory

Downtown and Northern Rio

Mid-Range
Ibis Rio de Janeiro Centro

Baia de Guanabara

Budget
Hotel Vitoria
Regina
Mid-Range
Glória Palace

Copacabana, Ipanema and Leblon

Budget
Augusto's Copacabana Hotel
Cabana Copa Hostel
Ipanema Bed and Breakfast
Mango Tree Hostal
Rio Hostel
Mid-Range
Arpoador Inn
Astoria
Olinda Othon Classic
Windsor Excelsior Hotel
Luxury
Fasano

Marina All Suites
Sofitel Rio de Janeiro

The Hills

Mid-Range
Rio 180° Hotel
Luxury
Mama Ruisa

Beach Suburbs

Mid-Range
Villaggio Mar a Mar Pousada Residencial

Further Afield

Mid-Range
Fazenda Florença
Pousada do Cais
Luxury
Casa Turquesa
Pedra da Laguna
Pousada da Alcobaça
Pousada Azeda
Pousada Insólito

Sleeping A–Z

PRICES

Prices are approximate and are based on a double room for one night.

$$$ over R$500
$$ R$200–R$500
$ under R$200

ARPOADOR INN $$

www.arpoadorinn.com.br
Right on the beach in between Ipanema and Copacabana, this hotel may not be the most

modern or the most luxurious in the city, but its location can't be beaten. Be sure to ask to see the rooms before committing, as they do vary.
🔲 E12 ✉ Rua Francisco Otaviano 177, Ipanema ☎ 2523 0060 🚇 Ipanema/General Osório

ASTORIA $$

www.redeatlantico.com.br/pt-br/astoria-copacabana
There's a small rooftop pool, a gym and sauna at this modern high-rise hotel in Copacabana. The upper

SLEEP

155

floors have views of the beach, three blocks away.
➕ F10 ✉ Rua República de Peru 345, Copacabana ☎ 2545 9090 🚇 Cardeal Arcoverde

AUGUSTO'S COPACABANA HOTEL $

www.augustoshotel.com.br
This hotel has clean, bright rooms, a small pool and a rooftop jacuzzi.
➕ E11 ✉ Rua Bolivar 119, Copacabana ☎ 2547 1800 🚇 Cantagalo

CABANA COPA HOSTEL $

www.cabanacopa.com.br
A few blocks from Copacabana beach in a safe, quiet area, this hostel has dorms and some rooms with private bathrooms. It's popular with backpackers.
➕ F9 ✉ Travessa Guimarães Natal 12, Copacabana ☎ 3988 9912 🚇 Cardeal Arcoverde

CASA TURQUESA $$$

www.casaturquesa.com.br
A breathlessly chic boutique hotel, Casa Turquesa faces Paraty's harbourside and has immaculately designed decor and temple-like serenity. The polished wooden flooring throughout the restored

18th-century *pousada* contrasts with the cool white walls. There are nine individually styled rooms, some with four-poster beds; also a plunge pool and spa.
➕ Map, ▷ 110 ✉ Rua Dr Pereira 50, Paraty ☎ (24) 3371 1037 🚌 Take a taxi from the bus station or a 15-min walk

FASANO $$$

www.fasano.com.br
Fasano is possibly the coolest hotel in Rio, discreetly tucked at the Copacabana end of Ipanema beach. Inside Philippe Starck's simple modern block is a space-age interior, full of dark woodwork, translucent drapes, floor lighting, blob-shaped mirrors and pop art furniture. The rooms and suites have a balcony, king-sized bed and large flat-screen TV. There's also the superb Fasano Al Mare restaurant (▷ 147) and Baretto Londra (▷ 131), plus a rooftop infinity pool with views.
➕ D12 ✉ Avenida Vieira Souto 80, Ipanema ☎ 3202 4000 🚇 Ipanema/General Osório

FAZENDA FLORENÇA $$

www.hotelfazendaflorenca.com.br
In a beautiful old coffee plantation in the Vale do Café, the large rooms, with a balcony, overlook pretty gardens. Excellent buffet meals are served and facilities in the spacious grounds include two pools, a tennis court and kids' club.
➕ Map, ▷ 110 ✉ Estrada da Cachoeira 1560, Conservatória ☎ (24) 2438 0124 🚌 2 hours by bus from Rio

GLÓRIA PALACE $$

www.hotelgloriario.com.br
One of Rio's grand old dames, the Glória Palace opened in 1922 and was extensively renovated in

SLEEP

2011. Overlooking the marina and next to Glória's lovely church, it offers old-style service and charm.

⊞ G4 ✉ Praia do Russel 632, Glória ☎ 2205 7972 ⏱ Due to reopen at the end of 2011, after renovations 🚇 Glória

HOTEL VITORIA $
Opposite the Palácio do Catete (▷ 71), this modern hotel is in the heart of this popular residential area between the city centre and Zona Sul. It offers clean, secure rooms, with helpful staff.

⊞ G5 ✉ Rua do Catete 172, Flamengo ☎ 2205 5397 🚇 Catete

IBIS RIO DE JANEIRO CENTRO $$
www.hotelibis.com.br
This is a good choice downtown, an area not well supplied with decent hotels. The rooms are quite basic, but are clean and good value.

⊞ F3 ✉ Rua Silva Jardim 32, Centro ☎ 3511 8200 🚇 Carioca

IPANEMA BED AND BREAKFAST $
A friendly family runs this clean, comfortable B&B, on a quiet

The restaurant at the Fasano hotel

street a short walk from the beach, by *posto* 9. The breakfasts are excellent.

⊞ C12 ✉ Rua Joana Angélica 61/201, Ipanema ☎ 9210 7531 🚇 Ipanema/ General Osório

MAMA RUISA, SANTA TERESA $$$
www.mamaruisa.com
This is an arty little boutique hotel in a colonial villa on a quiet Santa Teresa side street. French owner Jean Michel Ruis has created a glamorous retro style, with each room decorated in tribute to a screen or stage icon. Breakfast is served on a balcony with city views and there's a pool in the lovely walled garden.

⊞ F4 ✉ Rua Santa Cristina 132, Santa Teresa ☎ 2242 1281 🚃 Tram to Largo dos Guimarães

MANGO TREE HOSTAL $
www.mangotreehostal.com
There's a lively, backpacker atmosphere at this hostel, in a pretty villa that has cosy little rooms, a lounge and a small backyard with barbecue area. There's free WiFi.

⊞ D12 ✉ Rua Prudente de Morais 594, Ipanema ☎ 2287 9255 🚇 Ipanema/ General Osório

MARINA ALL SUITES $$$
www.hoteismarina.com.br
This tall modern block on Leblon seafront has a range of suites, including deluxe designer rooms favoured by celebs. Its restaurant and romantic Bar d'Hotel cocktail bar (▷ 131) also attract the local jet set. There's a small rooftop pool, a gym and a sauna.

⊞ B12 ✉ Avenida Delfim Moreira 696, Leblon ☎ 2172 1100 🚌 175, 177, 382

OLINDA OTHON CLASSIC $$

www.hoteis-othon.com.br
This elegantly designed medium-sized hotel, facing the centre of Copacabana beach, opened in 1949. Some of the stylish rooms have a balcony and view, and there's a spacious lobby and lounge areas.
➕ F10 ✉ Avenida Atlântica 2230, Copacabana ☎ 2159 9000 Ⓢ Siqueira Campos

PEDRA DA LAGUNA $$$

www.pedradalaguna.com.br
In Búzios, overlooking Praia da Ferradura, this pretty boutique hotel has a tennis court and pool with stunning shady terrace. The bedrooms are spacious, some with jacuzzis, and two are adapted for guests with disabilities.
➕ Map, ▷ 111 ✉ Rua 6, Lote 6, Quadra F, Praia da Ferradura, Búzios ☎ (22) 2623 1965 ▣ Taxi from bus station

POUSADA DA ALCOBAÇA $$$

www.pousadadaalcobaca.com.br
This delightful 19th-century villa is in gorgeous gardens close to Petrópolis. The spacious rooms are beautifully furnished. The grounds have an outdoor pool, tennis court and scenic trail around the perimeter, next to a roaring river. The excellent restaurant is run by Dona Laura Góes (▷ 149) and is open to non-residents.
➕ Map, ▷ 110 ✉ Rua Agostinho Goulão 298, Correias ☎ (24) 2221 1240 ▣ 15 min by taxi from Petrópolis bus station

POUSADA AZEDA $$$

www.pousadaazeda.com.br.
Enjoy great views over Azeda, João Fernandes and Ossos beaches from this hilltop boutique hotel at the tip of the Búzios peninsula. The 18 rooms and suites are prettily decorated with modern art and furniture, and there's a pool, gym, restaurant and bar.
➕ Map, ▷ 111 ✉ Rua João Fernandes 101, Búzios ☎ (22) 2623 5444 ▣ 10 min by taxi from bus station

POUSADA DO CAIS $$

www.pousadadocais.com
On Paraty's waterfront, by the church of Santa Rita, this colonial *pousada* has simple but tastefully furnished rooms, some with views. There's also a courtyard garden.
➕ Map, ▷ 110 ✉ Travessa Santa Rita 20, Paraty ☎ (24) 3371 1200 ▣ 5 min by taxi from bus station or 20-min walk

POUSADA INSÓLITO $$$

www.insolitos.com.br
This stunning boutique hotel is in manicured grounds on a secluded section of Ferradura beach. The individually themed rooms and suites have luxurious furnishing, with a tasteful mix of ethnic and modern art. There are several pools, lounges, restaurants and bars, and occasional live music. Children are not allowed as there

SLEEP

are steep steps and the focus is on a romantic ambience for couples.

🔲 Map, ▷ 111 ✉ Rua E1, Lote 3 & 4, Condomínio Atlântico, Praia da Ferradura, Búzios ☎ (22) 2623 2172 🚖 Taxi from bus station

REGINA $

www.hotelregina.com.br

A cut above the usual standard in this backpackers' area, Regina has mod-cons in clean rooms, including air conditioning, a mini-bar and TV. There's a terrace and massage suite on the seventh floor. It's one block from the beach on a quiet side street.

🔲 G5 ✉ Rua Ferreira Viana 29, Flamengo ☎ 3289 9999 🚇 Catete

RIO 180° HOTEL $$

www.rio180hotel.com

This chic hotel in Santa Teresa is named for its sweeping views over the city centre and Corcovado. The modern suites are individually designed and there's a pool, spa, sauna and highly rated restaurant.

🔲 E6 ✉ Rua Dr Júlio Otoni 254, Santa Teresa ☎ 2205 1247 🚇 Tram to Largo dos Guimarães or taxi

RIO HOSTEL $

www.riohostelipanema.com

Very popular with backpackers, Rio Hostel is in a small villa on a quiet residential street. It has clean rooms, a cheery top-floor deck with hammocks and a small front yard.

🔲 E11 ✉ Rua Canning 18, Casa 1, Ipanema ☎ 2287 2928 🚇 Ipanema/ General Osório

SOFITEL RIO DE JANEIRO $$$

www.accorhotels.com.br

This large modern hotel dominates the far end of Copacabana beach, with great views from its terraces and seafront rooms with balconies. The excellent facilities include two pools, and the service is impeccable. The top-class restaurant, Le Pré Catelan (▷ 150), is run by French chef Roland Villard.

🔲 E12 ✉ Avenida Atlântica 4240, Copacabana ☎ 2525 1232 🚇 Cardeal Arcoverde

VILLAGGIO MAR A MAR POUSADA RESIDENCIAL $$

www.villaggiomaramar.com.br

Opposite Recreio dos Bandeirantes beach, this self-catering chalet hotel is handy for surfers. There are seven chalets, with cooking facilities, TV, internet and air conditioning.

🔲 Map, ▷ 104 b5 ✉ Estrada do Pontal, 6516, Recreio ☎ 3411 1029 🚌 702, 703 from Barra da Tijuca

WINDSOR EXCELSIOR HOTEL $$

www.windsorhoteis.com.br

One of the best mid-range hotels on Copacabana beach has a reputation for attentive service. There are more than 200 rooms and suites, with all mod-cons, and a huge buffet breakfast.

🔲 F10 ✉ Avenida Atlântica 1800, Copacabana ☎ 2195 5800 🚇 Cardeal Arcoverde

---

LUXURY LIVING

For that special occasion, the Brazilian Beach House company (www.brazilian beachhouse.com) offers top-of-the-range rented houses in Ipanema, Paraty and Santa Teresa, some including the services of a chef, driver and valet/butler. The properties are immaculately furnished and fitted with the best hi-tech gadgets.

Need to Know

This section takes you through all the practical aspects of your trip to help it run more smoothly and give you confidence before you go and while you are there.

NEED TO KNOW

Planning Ahead

WHEN TO GO

Rio has a tropical climate, making it warm all year round. Being tropical also means there is humidity and rainfall much of the year, particularly from October to March. The busiest tourist season is from mid-December to the end of February, when hotels and flights are booked far in advance. A better time to come is either from March to May or August to October, when the city is less crowded and temperatures are more comfortable.

TIME

Brazil has various time zones. Rio is on Brazilian standard time, three hours behind GMT. Clocks go forward one hour in October, making Rio two hours behind GMT. Brazilian standard time resumes in February.

TEMPERATURE

JAN	FEB	MAR	APR	MAY	JUN	JUL	AUG	SEP	OCT	NOV	DEC
28°C	28°C	27°C	25°C	25°C	23°C	22°C	23°C	23°C	24°C	25°C	26°C
82°F	82°F	81°F	77°F	77°F	73°F	72°F	73°F	73°F	75°F	77°F	79°F

Winter (May–Jul) is less humid and warm than other times of year, with dry days and cooler evenings.
Summer (Nov–Feb) is hot and humid during the day, with heavy rain usually daily. It remains warm at night.
Between these periods (Aug–Oct, Mar–Apr), days are warm but not so humid, and nights are more comfortable.

NEED TO KNOW

WHAT'S ON

January/February
Rei & Rainha da Praia (King & Queen of the Beach): international beach volleyball tournament, Ipanema.
February/March
Carnaval: world-famous spectacle featuring huge street parades, costumed dancers and giant floats. (For dates, ▷ 7.)
March *Founding of the city of Rio de Janeiro* (1 Mar): procession from the church of São Sebastião dos Capuchinhos, in Barra da Tijuca, to the Metropolitan Cathedral.

April *Dia do Índio* (19 Apr) celebration for Brazil's indigenous peoples, held at the Museu do Índio; exhibitions, dance, music and children's activities.
May/June *Rio das Ostras Jazz e Blues:* major music festival held in a coastal resort east of Rio (▷ 134).
July *Portas Abertas:* open studio art festival in Santa Teresa, plus street parties and foodstalls (▷ 137).
FLIP: literary festival in Paraty, attracting leading writers.
September
Independence Day (7 Sep):

downtown military parade, and city-wide sports and cultural celebrations.
October *Nossa Senhora Aparecida & Children's Day* (12 Oct): patron saint's holiday, plus children's events and activities across the city.
November *Noites Cariocas:* live music festival featuring top Brazilian artistes, throughout the summer at Pier Maua.
December *New Year's Eve* (31 Dec): huge celebrations, with fireworks and a beach party in Copacabana.

RIO ONLINE

www.rioguiaoficial.com.br
The city's official tourist guide offers a range of information in English, from tours and restaurants to events and culture.

www.rio.rj.gov.br
The city council website gives an overview of Rio's districts and tourist attractions, as well as what's-on and accommodation listings.

www.turisrio.rj.gov.br
Tourist information for Rio de Janeiro state, covering Búzios, Niterói, Petrópolis, Paraty and other places within a few hours' travel.

www.braziltour.com
The Brazilian Institute of Tourism website, with useful information about the whole country, including events and special interest activities.

www.rio-carnival.net
Find out all about the world's most famous carnival, with online booking facilities.

http://vejabrasil.abril.com.br/rio-de-janeiro
An online version of the glossy magazine (Portuguese only), with arts listings, nightlife, restaurants, sport, fashion and society gossip.

www.riothisweek.com
An arty guide to Rio and São Paulo, with travel tips, news and culture features, plus music, nightlife and restaurant reviews.

www.rcvb.com.br
This Rio guide has useful information for business visitors, including hotel listings.

http://riotimesonline.com
Rio's English-language news website, with travel tips and an events calendar.

www.trilhasdorio.com.br
Website of an adventure travel company, with information (Portuguese only) on walks in Tijuca Forest and other parks near Rio.

USEFUL TRAVEL SITES

www.theAA.com
An excellent source of travel tips, ranging from worldwide destination information to travel insurance policies. You can also order AA's worldwide travel guides and maps online (UK only).

www.fodors.com
The complete website for travel planning. You can research prices and weather; book flights, car rental and holiday accommodation; exchange questions and answers with fellow travellers; it also has useful links to other sites.

INTERNET CAFÉS

Rates in internet cafés are usually around R$2 per 30 minutes. Many hotels also offer free internet access to their guests (with WiFi zones if you have your own laptop). Internet cafés include:

Central Fone
Handy if you're travelling.
✉ Carioca Metrô Station, Centro ☎ 2220 3841
🕐 Mon–Fri 9.30–8.30

Jasmin Manga Cyber Café
One of the few cafés in Rio with free internet connection, this place also serves a decent cup of coffee and tasty cakes.
✉ Paschoal Carlos Magno 143, Largo do Guimarães, Santa Teresa ☎ 2242 2605
🕐 Wed–Mon 10am–midnight

Getting There

ENTRY REQUIREMENTS

● Foreign passport-holders will be given an immigration form to complete on arrival; keep this safe with your passport as it needs to be handed in on departure (a fine may be charged if you lose it).

● US and Canadian passport holders need a visa to enter Brazil; apply at your nearest consular office. UK and most other EU nationals do not need a visa (exceptions include nationals of Cyprus, Estonia, Latvia and Malta, who do need a visa). Other nationalities should check with the Brazilian embassy in their home country. Always check entry requirements before you travel as they can change at short notice.

● Tourists are allowed to stay for up to 90 days, a period which may be extended at the discretion of the Polícia Federal. Your passport must be valid for at least six months, and authorities may ask to see your return air ticket and proof of sufficient funds.

● Although Rio is not within a yellow fever risk zone, a yellow fever certificate must be shown if you have visited affected countries up to three months before your visit; check with your local health service before departure, and note that yellow fever vaccinations take 10 days to become effective.

AIRPORTS

Antônio Carlos Jobim International Airport (www. infraero.com.br), Rio's international airport (GIG, still often called by its former name, Galeão), lies 20km (12 miles) north of the city. There are two terminals. Most airlines use Terminal One, particularly inter-continental flights. Terminal Two mostly serves domestic routes, as well as other international airlines.

Antônio Carlos Jobim International Airport

● Rio

48km (30 miles) • 32km (20 miles) • 16km (10 miles)

FROM ANTÔNIO CARLOS JOBIM INTERNATIONAL AIRPORT

Many US and European airlines fly to Rio, with most connecting via São Paulo (Guarulhos—GRU). Flights from London take approximately 11 hours, and flights from New York take around 10 hours. The two main Brazilian airlines are TAM (www.tam.com.br) and Gol (www.voegol.com.br). For airport information, tel 3398 5050.

The airport is well connected to the city by road, with freeways linking to Avenida Brasil, downtown and on to the Zona Sul, for the main tourist districts. It takes about 45 minutes to reach Copacabana and up to 1 hour to Barra. Regular (yellow-and-blue) taxis are plentiful, charging an average of R$40 to Copacabana and R$50 to Ipanema; they operate on a meter, which is generally reliable. Alternatively, there are radio-taxi stands in the arrivals terminal, where you can buy a fixed-fare voucher, costing around R$70 to the Zona Sul.

The REAL air-conditioned bus (tel 0800 240850) offers a reliable and cheap alternative to the city centre and on to Barra via Zona

Sul, every half hour from 5.30am to midnight (cost R$7). Or the airport shuttle bus service (tel 7842 2490; www.shuttlerio.com.br) goes direct to all the major hotels from Copacabana to Barra, costing R$9–R$17.

Inside the airport, there are tourist information desks, including the official city tourism authority, RIOTUR. You'll also find bureaux de change *(câmbio),* ATMs, a post office *(correio)* and a left-luggage deposit, as well as shops and restaurants.

CAR HIRE
Fast, reckless driving, a confusing road system, scarce safe parking sites and intimidating traffic police do not add up to make Rio the ideal city for independent driving. If you'd like to drive during your stay, however, the full range of international car rental agencies is available, plus several Brazilian companies. These include: Localiza (tel 0800 979 2000; www.localiza.com.br) and Unidas (tel 2240 6715; www.unidas.com.br).

INSURANCE
You are strongly advised to take out comprehensive insurance to cover your visit, including protection against loss and theft, as well as illness and accident. Check your current policy and buy supplementary cover if necessary. Although private medical care in Brazil is readily available, especially in cities, and of a high standard, treatment is expensive. The Brazilian public health service will care for you in an emergency, even without insurance, but the facilities are limited and basic.

SECURITY CONTROLS
As with air travel worldwide since 9/11, there are strict controls on what you can carry onto your flight in your hand luggage departing from Brazil. Check before setting off.

VACCINATIONS
Discuss with your doctor before your trip whether any vaccinations or other health precautions are advised.

CUSTOMS

● Visitors over 18 years old can purchase up to US $500 of duty-free products, including alcohol and tobacco, both on arrival in and departure from Rio. The airport's duty-free stores accept all major international currencies and credit cards, but not Brazil's own currency, the *real*.

● In addition to personal belongings, passengers may also bring in the following items: radio, CD player, laptop or notebook computer, movie and still camera.

● Import restrictions are imposed for fresh fruit, vegetables, seeds and other agricultural products.

● For full details of current regulations, check with the Brazilian Embassy:
UK: ☎ 0207 399 9000; www.brazil.org.uk
US: ☎ 202/238-2805; www.brasilemb.org
Canada: ☎ 613/237-1090; www.brasembottawa.org

TOURIST OFFICES

● RIOTUR (city tourism authority) ☎ 2271 7000; www.rioguiaoficial.com.br.
● Turisrio (Rio de Janeiro state tourism authority) ☎ 0800 282 2007; www.turisrio.rj.gov.br
● RIOTUR has information desks in the international airport, *posto* 6, Copacabana, and Rodoviária Novo Rio bus station.

Getting Around

VISITORS WITH DISABILITIES

● Some new hotels have low-level access for wheelchair users, but Rio is not especially well adapted for visitors with disabilities. Certain Metrô stations (marked with wheelchair symbols on the map) have special facilities, but city buses are not well suited for passengers with disabilities.
● Cooperativa Especial Cooptaxi is a specialized taxi service with cars adapted for passengers with limited mobility (☎ 3295 9606).

USEFUL BUS ROUTES

● Centro–Copacabana–Ipanema: 123, 125, 132
● Copacabana–Catete/Flamengo: 570, 572, 573
● Ipanema–Centro: 123, 132, 175
● Jardim Botânico–Centro: 170, 172, 179
● Jardim Botânico–Ipanema–Copacabana: 570, 572
● Lapa–Catete/Flamengo–Botafogo–Copacabana: 571
● Laranjeiras (Corcovado train)–Copacabana–Ipanema/Leblon: 570, 584
● Maracanã–Copacabana–Ipanema: 464
● São Conrado–Barra–Centro: 175, 177, 179
● Urca (Sugarloaf)–Copacabana–Ipanema–Leblon–Jardim Botânico: 512
● www.rioonibus.com has route details in its Guia de Itinerários (Portuguese only).

METRÔ RIO

Rio's Metrô (www.metrorio.com.br/en) is modern, fast, efficient, cheap and, best of all, the trains are air-conditioned. It is generally safe, though you're advised to avoid rush hours and late nights, especially in the quieter areas. MetroBus connections link to bus services, including the MetroBus service from Largo Machado to Cosme Velho for the cogtrain to Corcovado. There are two Metrô lines, with trains running to the central stations Monday to Saturday 5am–midnight, and Sunday 7am–11pm. Both lines cover Centro and on to Zona Sul via Flamengo and Botafogo, as far as Ipanema (Praça General Osório). Line 1 starts in Saens Pena, in Tijuca, and Line 2 goes up to Pavuna, in Zona Norte.

The cost of a single journey (unitário) is R$2.80. Combined Metrô/bus tickets cost from R$3.60–R$4.40. A pre-paid card is also available, saving you time queuing at ticket offices, with a minimum charge of R$10. Some stations accept bicycles, which can be taken on the trains at weekends and on public holidays.

CITY BUSES

All corners of the city are well served by the comprehensive Rio Ônibus network (www.rioonibus.com), with buses running daily from early until late. First-time visitors may be a bit intimidated, as Rio's bus drivers have a reputation for fast, reckless driving, and the buses are sometimes a target for thieves. If you avoid rush hours and apply common sense, though, leaving valuables and jewellery in your hotel, they are well worth the effort.

There are not always bus stops; look out for groups of people waiting, usually on street corners. Bus numbers and destinations are clearly marked on the front. Single journeys range from R$2.50–R$3.50; keep change handy and pay as you enter, via a turnstile (not suitable for large luggage). RioCard is a pre-paid swipe card with an ID photo, though it's mostly useful only for long-stay visitors and residents.

TRAMS

The cheapest and most characterful public transport option in the city is the open-sided yellow trams (known as *bondes*—pronounced bon-jees), with wooden seats. These lurch, shake and rattle their way from downtown, over the historic Arcos da Lapa, and up through Santa Teresa's cobblestone lanes. There are two lines operating from the tram station near Carioca Metrô station, off Rua Senador Dantas. Both lines cover Santa Teresa: one to Dois Irmãos and the other to Paula Mattos. Locals jump on and hang onto the sides for a free ride; leave your valuables behind and keep hold of bags in front of you. Trams run daily every half hour, 6.40am–8.40pm (guided tours on Saturdays at 10am and noon, R$4). Tickets cost R$0.55 one-way.

TAXIS

The taxis you'll see most on Rio's streets are the standard yellow-and-blue-striped cars. The metered fares are reasonable, and drivers are generally honest and helpful. The two-tier rates are indicated by the number on a little flag over the meter on the dashboard: up to 10pm is level 1; after 10pm and all-day Sundays and public holidays is level 2, which is 20 per cent more expensive. For the extra convenience of pre-booking, however, there are also radio taxis, which are painted with a red-and-yellow stripe. Radio taxis, air-conditioned and generally newer, also operate a meter system, but cost about 30 per cent more than the standard cabs. Among the best-known companies are Transcoopass (tel 2590 2300), Coopertramo Radiotaxi (tel 2560 2022/2200 9292) and Coopatur Radiotaxi (tel 2573 1009/3885 1000).

OLYMPIC IMPROVEMENTS

Barra will host the Olympic Village in 2016 and improvements are being made to the public transport system. Around R$4 billion will be spent on the Metrô, extending it to Jardim Oceânico, at the eastern end of Barra. A rapid transit bus service is also planned.

TOURS

Tour options include:
Culture and History
Carlos Roquette ☎ 9911 3829, www.culturalrio.com.br
Favelas Marcelo Armstrong, Favela Tours (▷ 73)
Tijuca National Park Rio Hiking ☎ 2552 9204/9721 0594, www.riohiking.com.br; Rio Trilhas ☎ 9779 0780, www.riotrilhas.com.br; and Trilhas do Rio ☎ 2424 5455/ 2425 8441, www.trilhasdorio. com.br.

WALKING

With its miles of soft, sandy beaches, peaceful parks and gardens, and embraced by the huge tropical forest of Tijuca National Park, Rio is a fantastic place for walkers. Guided walks are available (▷ above), offering local insights on the city's cultural and historical make-up.

MAPS

RIOTUR, the official tourism authority, produces free maps, which are widely available at tourist information kiosks in the international airport, downtown and throughout Zona Sul. Many hotels also provide street maps for their guests. Quatro Rodas, the national motoring organization, publishes the excellent annual *Guia 4 Rodas* (in Portuguese and English), which includes a map, guidebook and CD.

Essential Facts

ETIQUETTE

● *Cariocas* dress casually for all but the most formal occasions. Take an extra layer of clothing if you're going somewhere smart in the evening, as air-conditioning systems can be ice cool.
● Nudity on the beach is not customary in Rio, although Praia Abricó, to the west of Barra, is a small beach that is popular with naturists.
● Most restaurants include a service charge *(taxa de serviço)* in the bill; otherwise 10 per cent is the norm.
● Smoking is prohibited on public transport. A few restaurants have non-smoking areas but smoking is more accepted in Brazil than in some other countries.

PUBLIC TOILETS

There are very few public toilets in Rio, outside of airports and the main bus station. Most hotels and restaurants won't mind you using their facilities, however.

POSTAL SERVICES

The Brazilian postal service *(Correio)* is reasonably reliable, if slow. International courier companies have offices in Rio, or SEDEX is the express door-to-door service available at major post offices. Bright yellow post boxes are widespread, or larger hotels sell stamps and will post cards for you.

CONSULATES

● Australia: Avenida Presidente Wilson 231, 23rd floor, Centro, tel 3824 4624
● Canada: Atlântica Business Center, Avenida Atlântica 1130, fifth floor, Copacabana, tel 2543 3004
● UK: Praia do Flamengo 284, second floor, Flamengo, tel 2555 9600
● US: Avenida Presidente Wilson 147, Centro, tel 3823 2000

ELECTRICITY

Rio uses 110 or 120 volts AC; most hotels use both and sometimes 220V. Sockets take twin-pronged plugs, either flat- or round-pin.

EMERGENCY HOSPITALS

● Lourenço Jorge, Avenida Ayrton Senna 2000, Barra da Tijuca, tel 3111 4680
● Miguel Couto, Avenida Bartolomeu Mitre 1108, Gávea, tel 3111 3800/3685/3689
● Rocha Maia, Rua General Severiano 91, Botafogo, tel 2295 2295

EMERGENCY PHONE NUMBERS

Police: 190
Fire/ambulance: 193

MEDICAL TREATMENT

The public health service provides emergency care for non-Brazilians free of charge, but the facilities are basic. Make sure your personal insurance policy covers private medical treatment. There are several good private hospitals and dentists in Rio, but they are not cheap.

MEDICINES

Pharmacies *(farmacias)* are widespread, but bring your prescription with a note from your doctor if you need to buy medicine in Rio.
● Farmácia do Leme (24 hours), Avenida Prado Junior 237/A, Leme, tel 2275 3847

MONEY MATTERS

The Brazilian currency is the *real* (R$, plural *reais*). There are 100 *centavos* to the *real*, with 5, 10, 20, 50 and 100 *real* notes. Most major international credit cards are accepted, but check with your bank that your card can be used in Brazil and find out the charges. There are many ATMs—use those inside banks rather than on the street. Bureaux de change *(casas de câmbio)* also change foreign currency. US dollars are no longer widely accepted and traveller's cheques are very rarely used.

NATIONAL HOLIDAYS
- 1 Jan: New Year's Day
- Shrove Tuesday
- Good Friday
- 21 Apr: *Tiradentes*
- 1 May: Labour Day
- 7 Sep: Independence Day
- 12 Oct: Our Lady Aparecida
- 2 Nov: All Souls' Day
- 15 Nov: Republic Day
- 24 Dec: Christmas Eve
- 25 Dec: Christmas Day

OPENING HOURS
- Banks: Mon–Fri 10–4
- Offices: Mon–Fri 9–6
- Post offices: Mon–Fri 8–6, Sat 8–noon
- Shopping malls: Mon–Sat 10–10 (the largest malls also open Sun 3–9)
- Shops: Mon–Fri 9–7, Sat 9–1
- Supermarkets: Mon–Sat 8am–10pm (a few also open on Sun or are open 24 hours)

SENSIBLE PRECAUTIONS
Petty crime does occur in Rio, but the risks can be minimized with a few precautions:
- Most hotel rooms have a safe—use it.
- Bring photocopies of your passport and other valuable documents, and keep them in a separate place from the originals.
- Avoid downtown (Centro) at weekends and after dark.
- Never visit a *favela* (shanty town) alone, only with a recommended guide.
- Keep your valuables safely out of sight when out and about; dress down to be inconspicuous.

TELEPHONES
- Calls are expensive, especially if calling abroad from your hotel room.
- The area code for Rio and Niterói is 21. You do not need to dial this if you are calling from within the area.
- International direct dialling (DDI) is possible from blue public phone boxes, which use phone cards, sold at newsstands and post offices.
- To call abroad, dial 00, then the country code, the area code and the phone number. Leave out the zero if the area code starts with zero.
- For the international operator (English-speaking) dial 000 333.

TOURIST POLICE
✉ DEAT, Rua Humberto de Campos 315, Leblon
☎ 2332 2924 🕐 24 hours
The tourist police, who speak English, help visitors who have been victims of robbery or an accident, who may need a report for insurance claims.

TIPS
- You are advised to drink bottled water.
- Mosquitoes are prevalent, particularly in the wet season. Use repellent and wear long sleeves and trousers in the early evening and morning.

Words and Phrases

Even if you're far from fluent, it is always a good idea to try to speak a few words of Brazilian Portuguese. The words and phrases here should help you with the basics, from reserving a hotel room to dealing with emergencies. Remember that if a word has an accent, this is where the stress falls.

FOOD AND DRINK

English	Portuguese
breakfast	café da manhã
lunch	almoço
dinner	jantar
snack	lanche
starters	entradas
main course	prato principal
dessert	sobremesa
drink	bebida
carbonated drink	refrigerante
beer	cerveja
wine	vinho
fruit juice	suco
coffee	café
tea	chá
milk	leite
fruit	fruta
knife	faca
fork	garfo
spoon	colher
salt	sal
black pepper	pimenta do reino
chilli	pimenta
oil	azeite
bread	pão
sugar	açúcar
cheese	queijo
soups	sopas
steak	bife
fish	peixe
chips	batata frita
chicken	frango
barbecue	churrasco
well done	bem passado
sandwich	sanduíche
cod	bacalhau
sardines	sardinhas
rice	arroz

CONVERSATION

I don't speak Portuguese.	Não falo Português.
Do you speak English?	Fala Inglês?
I don't understand.	Não compreendo.
My name is ...	Meu nome é ...
Hello, pleased to meet you.	Olá, prazer em conhecê-lo(a).
I'm on holiday.	Estou de férias.
I live in ...	Vivo em ...
Good morning.	Bom dia.
Good afternoon.	Boa tarde.
Good evening/night.	Boa noite.
Goodbye.	Tchau.
See you later.	Até logo.
May I/Can I?	Posso?
How are you?	Tudo bom?
I'm sorry.	Desculpe.
Excuse me.	Com licença.
Where are the toilets?	Onde ficam os banheiros?

RESTAURANTS

I'd like to reserve a table for ... people at ...	Gostaria de reservar uma mesa para ... pessoas às ....
A table for ..., please.	Uma mesa para ..., por favor.
We have/haven't reserved.	Temos reserva/não temos reserva.
Is this table taken?	Esta mesa está ocupada?
Could we see the menu/ wine list?	Pode nos trazer um cardápio/lista dos vinhos?
Are there tables outside?	Há mesas lá fora?
We'd like something to drink.	Gostaríamos de tomar uma bebida.
Could I have bottled still/ sparkling water, please?	Pode me trazer uma garrafa de água sem gás/com gás, por favor?
I am a vegetarian.	Sou vegetariano(a).
I can't eat wheat.	Não posso comer trigo.
The bill, please.	A conta, por favor.

GETTING AROUND

Where is the timetable?	*Onde está o horário?*
Does this train/bus go to ...?	*Este trem/ônibus vai para ...?*
Do you have a Metrô/bus map?	*Tem um mapa do Metrô/dos ônibus?*
train/bus/Metrô station	*estação de trem/ terminal de ônibus/ estação de Metrô*
Where can I buy a ticket?	*Onde posso comprar um bilhete/passagem?*

HEALTH AND EMERGENCY

Help	*socorro*
stop	*pare*
emergency	*emergência*
police	*polícia*
dangerous	*perigoso*
accident	*acidente*
medicine	*remédio*
diarrhoea	*diarréia*
dehydration	*desidratação*
Keep out	*Mantenha distância.*
I don't feel well.	*Não me sinto bem.*
Can you call a doctor?	*Pode chamar um medico?*

ACCOMMODATION

Do you have a room?	*Tem um quarto?*
I have made a reservation for ... nights.	*Fiz uma reserva para ... noites.*
How much each night?	*Quanto é por noite?*
double room	*quarto de casal*
twin room	*quarto duplo*
single room	*quarto individual*
bathroom/toilet	*banheiro/toalete*
with bath/shower	*com banheira/choveiro*
Is there a lift in the hotel?	*O hotel tem elevador?*
Is the room air-conditioned?	*O quarto tem ar condicionado?*
Is breakfast/lunch/dinner included in the cost?	*O café da manhã/ almoço/jantar está incluído no preço?*
Is room service available?	*Tem serviço de quarto?*

NUMBERS

1	*um*
2	*dois*
3	*três*
4	*quatro*
5	*cinco*
6	*seis*
7	*sete*
8	*oito*
9	*nove*
10	*dez*
11	*onze*
12	*doze*
13	*treze*
14	*catorze*
15	*quinze*
16	*dezasseis*
17	*dezassete*
18	*dezoito*
19	*dezanove*
20	*vinte*
21	*vinte e um*
30	*trinta*
40	*quarenta*
50	*cinquenta*
60	*sessenta*
70	*setenta*
80	*oitenta*
90	*noventa*
100	*cem*

USEFUL WORDS

yes	*sim*
no	*não*
when	*quando*
why	*porquê*
how	*como*
later	*mais tarde*
now	*agora*
open	*aberto*
closed	*fechado*
please	*por favor*
thank you	*obrigado(a)*
big	*grande*
small	*pequeno*

Index

The Automobile Association would like to thank the following photographers, companies and picture libraries for their assistance in the preparation of this book.

Abbreviations for the picture credits are as follows – (t) top; (b) bottom; (c) centre; (l) left; (r) right; (AA) AA World Travel Library.

2i–6/7c AA/Julian Love; **6bl** AA/Yadid Levy; **6br–20/21t** AA/Julian Love; **20/21b** Corbis Super RF/Alamy; **21** Jeremy Sutton-Hibbert/Alamy; **22–37** AA/Julian Love; **38** Courtesy of Museu Casa do Pontal; **39** Courtesy of Museu Casa do Pontal; **40–42t** AA/Julian Love; **42b** Portinari, Candido / © DACS 2011; **42/43c–54/55t** AA/Julian Love; **54/55b** Photolibrary; **55** AA/Julian Love; **56** Ben Lewis/Alamy; **56/57t–57tr** AA/Julian Love; **57b** Ben Lewis/Alamy; **58l–59t** AA/Julian Love; **59b** echt/Alamy; **60–78** AA/Julian Love; **79t** Photolibrary; **79b–96** AA/Julian Love; **97t** Goncalo Diniz/Alamy; **97b–103** AA/Julian Love; **106t** Courtesy of Museu Casa do Pontal; **106c–160** AA/Julian Love.

Every effort has been made to trace the copyright holders, and we apologise in advance for any unintentional omissions or errors. We would be happy to apply any corrections in the following edition of this publication.

The author would like to thank the following people for their generous assistance, without which this book would not have been possible: Marcia Rabello, Miriam Cutz, Marcia Paula Migliacci, Sonia Mattos, Andrea Revoredo, Rob Shaw, Alex Malcolm, Simon Heyes, Suzana Wester, Michael 'Paddy' Smyth, Steven Chew, Bianca Teixeira, Vanessa Smith, João Vergara, DJ Zezinho, and Marcelo Armstrong. Plus, anyone else I may have forgotten to mention, including everyone at LATA, RioTur, RCVB, Turisrio, Jacada Travel, Senderos and Embratur.

Rio de Janeiro's 25 Best

WRITTEN BY Huw Hennessy
VERIFIED BY Jane Egginton
SERIES EDITOR Marie-Claire Jefferies
REVIEWING EDITOR Linda Schmidt
PROJECT EDITOR Kathryn Glendenning
COVER DESIGN Guido Caroti
DESIGN WORK Low Sky Design Ltd
INDEXER Joanne Phillips
IMAGE RETOUCHING AND REPRO Sarah Montgomery

ISBN 978-0-87637-145-9

FIRST EDITION

IMPORTANT TIP
Time inevitably brings changes, so always confirm prices, travel facts, and other perishable information when it matters. Although Fodor's cannot accept responsibility for errors, you can use this guide in the confidence that we have taken every care to ensure its accuracy.

SPECIAL SALES
This book is available for special discounts for bulk purchases for sales promotions or premiums. Special editions, including personalized covers, excerpts of existing books, and corporate imprints, can be created in large quantities for special needs. For more information, write to Special Markets/ Premium Sales, 1745 Broadway, 3-2, New York, NY 10019 or email specialmarkets@randomhouse.com.

Color separation by AA Digital Department
Printed and bound by Leo Paper Products, China

10 9 8 7 6 5 4 3 2 1

Cover image: John Foxx/Stockbyte/Thinkstock

A04923
Maps in this title produced from map data supplied by Global Mapping, Brackley, UK © Global Mapping/ITMB
Transport map © Communicarta Ltd, UK

Titles in the Series